OBJECT DETECTION UNDER POOR LIGHTING CONDITIONS USING DEEP LEARNING

SANATH S SHENOY

Final Thesis Report

DECEMBER 2021

DEDICATION

This Work is dedicated to my mother without whose encouragement and push I wouldn't have come so far to acquire knowledge and continuous learning

And

In the memory of my friend who always unconditionally supported and believed in me and my capabilities

ACKNOWLEDGMENT

I would like to thank Dr Vaibhav Kumar, Dr Rupal Bhargava and Dr Ahmed Kaky from Liverpool John More university for providing continuous guidance, sharing their valuable experiences and being the guiding light of my master's research work. Special thanks to Naveen Kumar Toppo and Seshu Babu VV Tolety, part of my department's Strategic and Business Management, who constantly supported me in my learning and research journey and helped balance my activities in my work front for this noble cause. I also heartily thank my organization, Siemens Technology and Services Limited, India, for strongly encouraging my learning and research journey during this challenging pandemic. I thank all the people who have directly or indirectly supported me in this research.

ABSTRACT

In recent years, there has been a lot of research done on object detection using deep learning. As a result, several real-time applications are being developed. These range from pedestrian detection, vehicle detection and counting, visual quality inspection in Industrial production and packaging, damage detection, and face recognition. These are being achieved by using different deep learning architectures such as Convolution Neural Networks and their extensions. Though there has been a lot of progress in these areas, object detection has been challenging in images with low light, poor visibility conditions. The solution to the mentioned scenario is important as it helps in use cases such as drone-based surveillance of important assets and human resources during floods, hurricanes and forest fires, accident avoidance in low light conditions and improvised detection capabilities in autonomous vehicles during rainy or cloudy conditions. The problem is tried to being solved in both traditional image processing and the use of deep learning. The research using deep learning approaches have been showing promising results. The proposed study evaluates a set of pretrained CNN-based deep learning models like YOLO, Fast RCNN, Faster RCNN, and SSD to choose the suitable deep learning model that can be reused or improvised. It also tries to understand different image processing methods, specifically enhancement techniques that can be used with the object detection deep learning models. Further, this can help detect the objects in low light poor visibility, with improved detection accuracy and speed.

TABLE OF CONTENTS

DEDICATION i
ACKNOWLEDGMENT ii
ABSTRACT...iii
LIST OF TABLES vii
LIST OF FIGURES viii
LIST OF ABBREVIATIONS ix

Chapter 1   INTRODUCTION 1
    1.1   Background of the Study 1
    1.2   Problems in Object Detection..2
    1.3   Problem Statement...3
    1.4   Research Question 4
    1.5   Aim and Objectives 4
    1.6   Scope of the Study 5
    1.7   Significance of the Study...5
    1.8   Structure of the Study 5

Chapter 2   LITERATURE REVIEW..7
    2.1   Introduction 7
    2.2   Object detection in Bad weather Rainy, Foggy and Hazy Condition............7
    2.3   Object detection In Marine Environments 10
    2.4   Object Detection of Pedestrians vehicles and Traffic Management 12
    2.5   Object Detection in Construction environments 14
    2.6   Object Detection for domestic and Military Surveillance 15
    2.7   Other Novel Approaches for Object detection 16
    2.8   Summary..20

Chapter 3   RESEARCH METHODOLOGY 21
    3.1   Introduction. 21
    3.2   Our Approach 21
    3.3   Dataset Description 23
    3.4   Dataset Selection 23
    3.5   Pre-processing 23

3.5.1	Denoising	23
	3.5.1.1 Median Filter	24
	3.5.1.2 Non-Local Mean Filter	24
	3.5.1.3 Laplacian filter	25
3.5.2	Image Contrast Adjustment	25
	3.5.2.1 Gamma Based Correction	25
	3.5.2.2 log-based Correction	26
	3.5.2.3 Histogram Equalization	26
	3.5.2.4 Contrast limited Histogram Equalization (CLAHE)	26
	3.5.2.5 Minmax Contrast Stretching	26
3.6	Use of Pretrained Models	27
3.7	Choice of pretrained models for the study	27
3.7.1	Yolo.	27
3.7.2	SSD	27
3.7.3	Fast RCNN	27
3.7.4	The Faster RCNN	28
3.8	Metric and evaluation of the new approach	28
3.9	Summary	28
Chapter 4	**IMPLEMENTATION AND ANALYSIS**	**30**
4.1	Introduction	30
4.2	Data Preparation and Preprocessing	30
4.2.1	Low light Image Identification	30
4.2.2	Image Resizing	31
4.2.3	Image Annotation	31
4.2.4	Description of classes for low light object detection	31
4.2.5	Ground Truth Processing	31
4.2.6	Distribution of Classes in the dataset	32
4.3	Selection of Pretrained Models and weights	32
4.4	Image Enhancement Techniques	33
4.5	Experimental infrastructure Setup	34
4.6	Experimental Scenarios	34
4.7	Measurement of Model Performance and Speed of Inference	36

	4.7.1 Confidence Score	36
	4.7.2 Intersection Over Union (IOU)	36
	4.7.3 Mean Average Precision (mAP)	36
	4.7.4 Prediction time	37
4.8	Summary	37

Chapter 5 RESULTS AND DISCUSSION 38

5.1	Introduction	38
5.2	Experiment without Enhancement Scenarios	38
5.3	Experiment with Enhancement Scenarios	38
5.4	Prediction Speed of Models with low light images	45
5.5	Summary	46

Chapter 6 CONCLUSION AND RECOMENDATIONS 47

6.1	Introduction	47
6.2	Discussion and Conclusion	47
6.3	Limitations	48
6.4	Contribution of Knowledge	48
6.5	Future Work	49

REFERENCES 50

APPENDIX A RESEARCH PLAN 57

APPENDIX B RESEARCH PROPOSAL 58

APPENDIX C CODE ON LOW-LIGHT OBJECT DETECTION 70

APPENDIX D ETHICS FORMS 71

LIST OF TABLES

Table 4.1 Pretrained models and their weights and presets 33
Table 4.2 Details of the experiments and their configurations 34
Table 5.1 Baseline experiment for low light images without enhancement at IOU=0.5 38
Table 5.2 Baseline experiment for low light images without enhancement at IOU=0.75 38
Table 5.3 Experiment with low light images with gamma correction at IOU=0.5 39
Table 5.4 Experiment with low light images with gamma correction at IOU=0.75 39
Table 5.5 Experiment with low light images with Histogram Equalization at IOU=0.50 41
Table 5.6 Experiment with low light images with Histogram Equalization at IOU=0.75 41
Table 5.7 Experiment with low light images with Contrast Stretching at IOU=0.50 43
Table 5.8 Experiment with low light images with Contrast Stretching at IOU=0.75 43
Table 5.9 Prediction time of models with low light images and enhancement techniques 45

LIST OF FIGURES

Figure 3.1 Flow chart of our Research methodology for low light object detection 22
Figure 3.2 Equation for median filter 24
Figure 3.3 Equations for Non-Local Mean Filter 25
Figure 3.4 Equation for Laplacian Filter 25
Figure 4.1 Ground truth Annotations converted to a Data frame 32
Figure 4.2 Distribution of object class in 125 low light images 32
Figure 5.1 Raw image, image with Gamma correction =1.5 40
Figure 5.2 Example image with objects detected after Gamma Correction 40
Figure 5.3 Raw image, Histogram equalized image 42
Figure 5.4 Example image with objects detected after Histogram Equalization 42
Figure 5.5 Raw image and minmax contrast stretched image 44
Figure 5.6 Example image with objects detected after Minmax Contrast Stretching 44
Figure A.1.0.1 Research Plan 57
Figure B.1.0.1 Flow chart of the Proposed Research Methodology 65
Figure B.1.0.2 Initial Research Plan 69

LIST OF ABBREVIATIONS

R-CNN ……. Recurrent Convolution Neural Network

CNN……... Convolution Neural Network

CPU ……… Central Processing Unit

CV………… Computer Vision

GPU……….. Graphics Processing Unit

GB ………… Giga Byte

LTS ………... Long Term Support

NN…………. Neural Network

PSNR………. Peak Signal-To-Noise Ratio

RAM……….. Random Access Memory

ROI ………… Region of Interest

RPN ………… Region Proposal Network

RGB………... Red Green Blue

SSD………… Single Shot Detector

SSH………… Secure Socket Host

SVM………... Support Vector Machine

VM…………. Virtual Machine

VNC………... Virtual Network Computing

YOLO……… You Look Only Once

Chapter 1 INTRODUCTION

This chapter gives a brief introduction to one of the most important field in the area of computer vision, known as object detection. It discusses the importance of object detection and the recent trends. It also provides a brief overview of how object detection was done in the past. Since the focus is on object detection using deep learning approaches, it provides an overview how different deep learning-based detectors and the important challenges faced by object detection as a whole. As part of this research, we strongly focus on low light object detection. The chapter elaborates on the key research questions and importance of low light object detection and how the research conducted in this line can serve towards the greater good of the society. We conclude the chapter by providing a brief overview of our research approach and finally how our thesis is organised where a top-level summary of all the chapters and their sections are provided.

1.1 Background of the Study

Object Detection is the most popular field of computer vision. Some applications of object detection include face detection, pedestrian detection, vehicle detection and tracking on the road. It is also being used extensively in self-driving cars and military drones. Object detection helps identify the type and location of the object in an image or a video. It also provides more information about the object so that the images and videos are understood well semantically (W. Liu et al., 2016). Object detection is also the first step towards advanced computer vision tasks as image or video segmentation, scene understanding, object tracking, image captioning and event detection(L. Liu et al., 2020).

The object detection methods can be classified into two types, namely traditional and deep learning-based methods(Zou et al., 2019). Some of the traditional methods to perform object detection include HOG Transform(Ballard, 1981), Harris Corner detection(Harris & Stephens, 1988) and SIFT(Lowe, 2004). HOG transform works using geometric feature extraction. Harris Corner detection extracts the corner features of two images and uses the correlation between them for detecting the objects. Finally, SIFT uses each feature in the image as an object. It also requires the calculation of key points associated with the location of the features and orientation of features. The algorithm is complex but very robust towards occlusion, rotation, or scaling(Zou et al., 2019). One potential drawback of the traditional methods is their strong dependence on feature engineering.

Currently, deep learning models are used extensively for object detection tasks. This is due to the rapid advancement of computational hardware like GPUs and growing interest in the area of computer vision for the use of deep learning methods. The deep learning methods use different variants of Convolution Neural Network for object detection. Depending on the number of stages to accomplish the detection tasks, there are two types of object detection models. They are single-stage and two-stage object detectors. The advantage of single-stage object detectors is that they can infer quickly, and the two-stage object detectors are good at accurate localisation and detection of objects(Jiao et al., 2019). examples of single stage detectors include YOLO (Redmon et al., 2016) and SSD (W. Liu et al., 2016). Similarly, examples of two-stage detectors include Fast RCNN(Girshick, 2015) and Faster RCNN(Ren et al., 2015). This study, however, only focuses on the use of deep learning-based methods with images that are taken under low light or poor visibility conditions using CNN variants such as YOLO, SSD, Faster-RCNN and Fast-RCNN.

Our research will be focused on low light object detection. It will be conducted in multiple stages. As the first step, we would create a dataset of low light images from various existing datasets. This includes choosing the low light images by visually inspecting the images one after the other from the Pascal VOC dataset, Reside dataset and the Disaster dataset. After this step, the images are checked with pretrained coco weights for YOLO, Faster RCNN and SSD to check the performance of object detection and speed. In the next stage, various image enhancement techniques are applied, and the step is repeated with pre-trained models. Once the most suitable model among the pre-trained model is identified, the performance of object detection and speed of the best model is observed. In the final step, we document our findings to conclude the study by listing out the steps and the identified reason behind the improvement

1.2 Problems in Object Detection

There are various challenges faced in object detection in both normal and low lighting conditions. These problems include the following

- Image of the same object captured in different orientations needs to extensively be studied so that they can be detected accurately in any orientation
- Objects are deformed; sometimes the same object changes its shape.
- Most of the objects in the real world are occluded, and this increases the complexity of detection with bad lighting conditions
- Occlusion also results in the detector failing to detect the objects or misclassifying them to a different object. Common examples in the low light scenario are classifying a dog to a horse, a car to a motorbike
- There can to many other objects present in the image that makes it complex to detect the actual object of interest
- Multiple categories of the same objects need to be detected correctly without misclassification. For example, cats come with different skin variations, but the detector has to detect it as a cat correctly. the problem with such a scenario is multi-fold with detection in low light
- Speed and reliability is the most critical aspect of object detection when dealing with real-time scenarios where detection is both time and life-critical.

However, the key challenges highlighted are currently solved by image processing techniques. The problem with image orientation is solved by the application of image augmentation(Jason Wang & Perez, 2017) and morphological transformation techniques. Deformed objects in the image are corrected using image registration techniques(Uchida, 2013). Finally, occlusion is a scenario where two or more objects in the image overlap. As a result, the view of the object in the background is blocked. This problem is treated using techniques such as inpainting(Chandler & Mingolla, 2016), diffusion, tracking and probabilistic approaches with limited success.

1.3 Problem Statement

As per (Zhiqiang & Jun, 2017), the object detection mechanism is limited by various factors such as noise, bad resolution, occlusion complex background and other conditions that affect the correctness of detection. Additionally, there has been very limited research on the use of deep learning models to detect objects under low light and unclear environmental conditions. In these scenarios, low light object detection can play a vital role in reducing a significant amount of human effort, the need for high-cost hardware and any other financial costs involved in detection monitoring and tracking, for example, in the context of traffic management and guided vehicles, object detection in low light can help avoid accidents on roads. It can help detect traffic rule violations on the roads even when there are average lighting conditions.

The key problem of our study is to understand object detection in poor lighting condition using deep learning. Another important aspect is to identify steps or methods that help improve object detection performance and speed by reusing the knowledge of existing models in the without having to train , but use of image processing methods like image enhancement, denoising etc.

1.4 Research Question

The research questions for the study are to understand the following

- How do standard deep learning object detection models perform the detection task in low light conditions?
- Can standard deep learning object detection models be reused, modified or combined for better object detection accuracy and speed under low light conditions?
- What are the other factors that contribute to the detection accuracy and speed of the deep learning models in low light conditions?

1.5 Aim and Objectives

The aim of this research is to propose the use of deep learning models to detect objects in poor lighting conditions.

The research objectives on the aim of this study are as follows:

- Preprocess the images so that they are suitable for object detection with the deep learning model.
- Identify the objects within an image using pre-trained deep learning models
- Systematically understand the performance of detection of general purpose pre-trained models in the context of poor or low light conditions.
- Compare the performance with at least three models to validate the detection performance and speed.

- Use at least three image processing / enhancement techniques along with pretrained general purpose object detection to see if they can improve the detection performance and speed in low light scenarios.

1.6 Scope of the Study

The scope of the research is to use deep learning-based models for object detection of images in poor lighting and bad weather conditions or any other low light condition. The study is limited to images that are taken in low light conditions. It also includes detection in hazy and bad visibility conditions taken from outdoors. It does not focus on object detection in dark spaces like deep ocean underwater lighting conditions, bad lighting conditions inside the natural caves or manmade buildings. It also does not focus on extremely dark and no light conditions or the lighting environments at a night setting. Additionally, the focus of the study is limited to the use of CNN based deep learning models such as YOLO, Faster RCNN, Fast RCNN and SSD and understanding their detection performance and speed when used with low light images.

1.7 Significance of the Study

The research tries to leverage the capability of computer vision and deep learning to identify objects of interest in images taken at low light or poor visibility conditions. It can be in various real-life scenarios. It can be used for remotely monitoring, tracking and decision making. This can help save time and resources. As the approach uses simple RGB images, it provides a potential low-cost alternative compared to sensor-based approaches. The research can also be deployed in unmanned drones for surveillance where lighting conditions are bad. It can also be used with self-driving vehicles to detect different objects of interest such as obstacles, signals humans and signs in low light conditions. These are some examples that clearly quantify the significance and benefits of the study, which in turn contribute to advancement in technology, save human life and time.

1.8 Structure of the Study

Our thesis is organised into different chapters. In the introduction chapter, we have already spoken about the background of our study which explains the broader areas of computer vision importance of low light object detection and its challenges. We have also further explained the broader methods of traditional hand-crafted and deep learning-based methods. This chapter further explains the problem statement, the scope, and the significance of the study. In the final part of the introduction section, we conclude by providing a gist of our approach to solve the problem of low light object detection. The second and most important part of our thesis is the literature survey. In this section, we try to understand the existing state of the art approaches in deep learning based low light object detection applied in different domains and understand their benefits and challenges. We also summarise the gaps and research opportunities to form the basis of our research method. The last important section of our thesis is the detailed explanation of our research methodology, where we elaborate the steps, the choice of the datasets, the preprocessing and image treatment methods and the choice of the models used. We also elaborate in brief the evaluation metric used to validate the approach. Some other sections of our thesis include the implementation and analysis of the research methodology, The discussion on the results of our experiments with pretrained models and image enhancement techniques. We also conclude and discuss the opportunities to improve in the future. Additionally, the addendum (annexure sections) includes the research plan and the research proposal prepared at the beginning of our study.

Chapter 2   LITERATURE REVIEW

2.1   Introduction

In this section we try to understand the different ways in which the problem of low light object detection was solved in the past using deep learning and convolution neural networks. The review tries to understand different domain-specific use cases under which the problem of low light is being solved. We also try to understand the techniques and their outcomes. The study not only analyses the standalone improvements of the deep learning models but also tries to understand novel methods of handling the image data such as image enhancement, denoising augmentation and techniques of preparing and generating training data. We try to understand different methods in which deep learning models are calibrated, trained, tuned, combined, extended, or fused to improve the object detection performance in various application domains. We organise the literature review based on use cases from different domains such as bad weather and hazy, low light condition, applications of low light object detection in marine and construction, pedestrian and traffic detection in low light, low light object detection in defence and so on. The details of each domain and their use case are explained in the following sections. We also capture the datasets of interest, salient improvements and novelties in the modelling or data processing approaches, important metrics and their drawbacks

2.2   Object detection in Bad weather Rainy, Foggy and Hazy Condition

(Singh & Singh, 2018) explain the main factors contributing to poor object detection performance with videos and images. These mainly include poor visibility, Hazy or fogginess in the image or the video. They suggest preprocessing the image using a guided filter and integrating Discrete Wavelet Transformation methods with the deep learning CNN architecture(Shin et al., 2016). The approach improves the detection performance by reducing the mean squared errors and improving the PSNR, Image information entropy significantly.

The work by (J.-G. Wang et al., 2018) solves the problem of object detection in bad weather conditions. The main challenge is when raindrops fall on the windshield makes the problem even more complex in autonomous vehicles. They also emphasize that sensor-based systems, including the radar give false positive detection. However, the authors consider the option of combining the sensor-based radar system with a vision based deep learning solution. The sensor provides an advantage of detecting obstacles easily from a far distance, whereas the deep learning model helps to localize and detect the obstacles very quickly. The model used for detection is YOLOV2. By using the detection results of the radar sensor and the object detection model, .it is possible to detect the obstacles accurately even under rainy and foggy conditions. Furthermore, it is also possible to calculate the distance of the vehicle from the obstacle. It is observed that by performing experiments on a large database of autonomous vehicles, the novel model is able to identify 99.995% of the cars from a distance of 180 meters. The acceptable frame rate at which the detection is working well is around 30- 40 frames per second. The experimental setup consists of a 2.5 GHz CPU with GTX 760 GPU to facilitate the object detection and distance(width) measurement. The width measurement performance also improved by five times using the new approach.

The authors(Y.-L. Wu et al., 2019) identify that datasets are available for normal weather and good lighting conditions for the object detection task. However, they highlight the scarcity of images with bad weather and poor lighting conditions. They also observe that models trained with normal weather and good lighting conditions do not perform well in the testing environment with bad weather or poor lighting conditions. To solve the problem. They modify the images with photoshop. The images are chosen from KITTI dataset and different types of images are created that represent the real environment with various weather and lighting conditions and then train different models. They train different models, including YOLO Faster RCNN, SSD. for training the SSD model, the images are compressed to have the same width and height. The experiments show that SSD performs better than all the other models. The accuracy detection during the daytime improved from 98.6% to 99.3% and the night detection accuracy increased from 22% to 50%.

The research(Volk et al., 2019) focuses on automated augmentation for training data to create a model which works in rainy conditions. These include scenarios like falling rain and rain drops on the windshields of vehicles. Synthetic images of different rain variations are generated. Additionally, the synthetic generated images are validated for noise behaviour such as Gaussian

Noise and salt and pepper noise. Datasets such as KITTI, Cityscapes is used to generate rainy conditions synthetically as it is difficult to gather real world rain images with different image variation on the actual road within a short time interval. The goal of the proposed research is to build a stable object detection model for vehicles on the road to work efficiently with real world rainy conditions. Results of the novel data augmentation technique used to train the deep learning models improved the performance with AP for Faster -RCNN by 4.37% and YOLOv3 by 7.33%.

The authors(Sindagi et al., 2020) try to solve the problem of Adverse weather conditions such as haze and rain, which alter the lighting and other qualities of the image result in object detection trained with clean images perform very poorly. They propose an unsupervised domain adversarial prior based object detection approach for detection in hazy and rainy conditions. for example, a hazy image is explained to be a super imposition of clean image and attenuated atmospheric lighting condition. Similarly, a rainy image is explained as the super imposition of rain residue on the clean image. This information specific to the weather or atmospheric condition results in degradation of the image qualities. These are also known as weather-specific priors. They also hypothesize that these weather-specific priors are directly correlated to the extent of degradation of image quality. To overcome these limitations, they try to make the image weather invariant by eliminating the weather-specific priors, that are responsible for image quality degradation. They also use knowledge of the weather-specific prior to the image to define a prior adversarial loss. The loss is minimized to mitigate the impact of weather conditions on detection performance. The approach is evaluated with Foggy-cityscapes, RTTS, and UFDD datasets. It is observed that the new approach performs significantly better than the recently available state of the art methods.

The research(Z. Zhang et al., 2020) tries to solve the problem of object detection in hazy conditions. It proposed a unified mechanism for Dehazing and detection. It uses a residual aware haze density classifier. This is combined with a haze density aware dehazing network and haze density aware object detector. The classifier predicts the density of haze in the hazy images. The knowledge of density is used by both the dehazing network and the object detector model. the dehazing method is known as HRDN. In this method, A high-resolution dehazing network is used to remove the haze from the image. After this the images are passed to Faster RCNN -based object detector. Experiments are performed on synthetic datasets. It is observed that the unified novel approach performs better than the existing approaches. Additionally, the detections in real-time hazy conditions are observed to work accurately.

The research(Le et al., 2020) focuses on object detection under low light and foggy conditions. The authors propose a novel CNN based model known as DFO-Net. The model contains two networks. The first network is responsible for defogging and generating a clean image, and the second network is responsible for object detection. The detection network uses the output image generated by the defogging network to localize and detect objects. The defogging process is mathematically represented as an atmospheric scattering model. A Faster-RCNN variant known as Retina net is used as an object detection model. The idea behind choosing retina net is that it can detect objects at different scales. It can also handle class imbalance during the training process. They use the FOD dataset to evaluate the model. The dataset contains 6000 images. The dataset is divided into a training set of 4200 images with 83572 object class instances validation set with 600 images with 12,358 object class instances and a test set with 12000 images having 24049 object class instances in the training data. It is observed that the newly developed model has an mAP of 45.85% for detection under foggy conditions. This is 0.87% better than plain retina net, 2.09% better than YOLOV3 and 3.2% better than SSD 512 model.

2.3 Object detection In Marine Environments

The research(Fu et al., 2018) focuses on detecting ships in the ocean. The faster RCNN network is trained with several different images of ships under different environmental and lighting conditions from a database of ships that were collected using different sources. The experiment is conducted to verify the performance of models. The authors explain that the detection performance is very good with clear images of ships with good lighting conditions. However, the network does not detect ships accurately in dim light and poor quality images. It is also observed that the network also does not detect small targets. To improve the performance of detection, different types of images containing small targets, reduced quality images, multi target and poor visibility images are introduced in the training dataset. The model retrained with new dataset having different combination of images increases the detection accuracy for ships of smaller sizes and different environmental conditions. They also identify that the robustness of the model increases. Finally, the paper concludes that the algorithm needs further improvements so that it is sensitive to target ships that are very small and ships with low visibility in complex environmental conditions.

(Nie et al., 2019) use YoloV3(Redmon & Farhadi, 2018) deep learning architecture to detect ships in bad weather. They try to understand whether Image enhancement techniques or a training technique with both good and bad weather images improve the detection performance. The findings help conclude that by combining degraded images and good images in the training phase, the model can improve the ship detection performance under bad weather significantly when compared to applying certain image enhancement techniques as a preprocessing step.

(Han et al., 2020)try to understand object detection in deep sea underwater low light conditions. It also identifies challenges such as weak illumination and poor-quality image that impact the object detection task under water. Due to the lack of image quality underwater two image enhancement methods namely max-RGB and shades of Grey method are used. An additional preprocessing state where a CNN is trained to understand the weekly illuminated part and extract the feature maps of the weekly illuminated parts of the image. Finally, A deep CNN based object detection method is used to detect the underwater objects. The proposed approach is compared with standard models such as YOLO V3, Fast RCNN and Faster RCNN. It is observed that the detection performance improved compared to the standard models. The mAP is observed to be 90% and the detection speed is 50 Frames per second. This approach clearly supports the hypothesis that the detection accuracy and speed can be improved to a greater extent by introducing image enhancement techniques and the additional preprocessing steps to extract weakly illuminated features before the actual object detection process using standard deep learning methods.

The research(Madhan et al., 2021) tries to solve challenges in underwater object detection system used in autonomous robots for underwater detection tasks. The study identifies that underwater images have bad illumination. They are blurred images that add to the complexity of the problem. The authors propose the use of well-known filters namely Gray shade and Max-RGB to improve the image quality. They also remove the image background. For bad illumination, CNN based approach for object localization and detection is used. The approach is compared with standard models such as SSD, YOLO, Fast RCNN and Faster RCNN. In the test setup, the new approach achieved a mapping score of 92% for an Intersection of Union configured at 0.8. The experimental setup is powered by NVIDIA GPU where the detection frame rate is at 30 Frames per second, and the detection time taken is 57 microseconds. All these results show that the new approach clearly performs better than classic models and already existing methods for object detection underwater submerged and poor lighting conditions.

(Asyraf et al., 2021) experiment with different YOLOv3 architecture variants to detect animals deep under the sea. They also highlight that the main challenge that can affect detection performance is degraded visibility in the image. As a result, the experiments are conducted by subjecting the images to preprocessing and augmentation. Different YOLO variants are trained and compared against each other to understand the detection capability of each model.

2.4 Object Detection of Pedestrians vehicles and Traffic Management

The work by (Lee & Shin, 2019) proposes the use of a deep learning-based object detection system with the tracking systems in the tunnel to minimize accidents and other undesirable events. The tracking system is combined with Faster RCNN. The system is connected to CCTV to aid automatic detection and monitoring. The monitoring system should keep track of four events, namely Wrong-Way driving, stop, human out of vehicle and fire incident. The object detection model is trained for three classes of objects namely car, person, and fire with different lighting conditions in the tunnel. The authors claim that the training average precision is achieved to be 0.8479 for car, 0.7161 for person and 0.9085 for fire. The accident detection system is tested with four accident videos captured by CCTV of the detection system. It is observed that the accident detection system is successful in detecting any accident in a duration as short as 10 seconds. Though the experiments conducted show good average precision in the training phase, the paper does not clearly provide more details on the average precision achieved at validation and test scenario. It also does not clearly quantify the detection performance in terms of the frame rate and the number of simultaneous objects detected and tracked in the real scenarios.

(G. Li et al., 2019) try to detect pedestrians in a hazy, low light image by modifying yolo deep learning architecture. It uses depth-wise convolution instead of the standard convolution technique. This helps to increase the speed of computation. It also uses a linear activation function instead of relu to minimise information loss. Additionally, a concept of priory boxes is introduced, which uses different sized boxes. The sizes are determined using K-Means(Likas et al., 2003) so that the network needs to learn to mark pedestrians or objects from the scratch. The modified architecture improved the detection performance by 4% from 79% to 83% and processing speed from 22 frames per second to 159 frames per second.

The paper(Hassaballah et al., 2020) tries to understand the key challenges faced by traffic tracking and surveillance systems. These include reduced visibility, fog, snow, rain, dust and sandstorm. The authors propose a three step approach to solve the problem, this illumination enhancement, reflection enhancement, and linear weight fusion. The idea involves combining white balancing for improving the image contrast. It also uses Gama correction for improving the illumination. It combines Laplacian Pyramid to enhance the reflection component. after these steps are applied to the image. It is introduced to CNN that uses Gaussian mixture probability hypothesis density filter, which is used for tracking in a combination of hierarchal data associations. The tracking loss is compensated using the Hungarian algorithm. The proposed method is tested with DAWN, KITTI and MS-COCO datasets. The experiments conducted show that that the proposed approach exceeds the performance of the state of art object detector GYOLOV3 for rain by 10.36%, snow by 13.94% and sandstorm scenario by 21.46%.

The study by(V. D. Nguyen et al., 2020) shows that the existing vehicle detection system is not accurate under different driving conditions, mainly in adverse weather, night light, rain, snow, lighting conditions in the tunnel, where lighting conditions are not normal. Moreover, hand-crafted feature-based methods like Local Binary Pattern (LBP) and Local Ternary Pattern (LTP) do not work well in poor lighting and bad driving conditions. Hence, they propose the use of an autoencoder to improve the performance of vehicle detection systems. It uses an unsupervised approach by introducing an auto encoder based deep learning approach to develop a transformation feature that can be used by object detectors to detect the obstacles and vehicles under difficult lighting conditions easily. The proposed auto encoder-based transformation approach is used with Faster R-CNN and YOLO. Experiments reveal that the object detection performance improved significantly when compared to the use of hand-crafted feature-based methods along with object detectors.

The paper(Zheng et al., 2021) aims to improve vehicle detection accuracy by using deep learning techniques. It also identifies the problem associated with vehicle detection like multi scale (images with different orientation), multi category (different types of vehicles) dim and minutely visible vehicles, similar vehicles with major and minor similarities, detection interference leading to an unacceptable or significant decrease in accuracy. An important objective of this approach is to avoid preprocessing. Hence it proposes the use of Fast R-CNN for vehicle detection in complex traffic scenarios. The structure of Fast-RCNN is also modified by replacing VGG16 with RESNET. This enhances the capability of the model to detect small targets with complex backgrounds. Max pooling is used as a down sampling method. Additionally, a Feature pyramid network is included as part of the Region proposal network to generate the candidate bounding box. The network is trained with 1497 images. The test result shows that the network is able to recognize the vehicles with an accuracy of 94.7%. The network is able to extract features of dim vehicles easily. One limitation of the approach is the long Training time even though it does not require any preprocessing step. This approach, however, performs far better than feature extraction methods that are designed manually.

(Lai et al., 2021) tries to improve pedestrian detection in low light conditions by modifying the Mask R-CNN(He et al., 2017) network. It introduces a fusion layer to enhance the region sensitivity and instance segmentation capability. As a result, the network's detection accuracy improves by 4.66%. The network is trained with varied image sizes and tested in a real environment as part of the electric vehicle to validate the finding.

(Z. Liu et al., 2020) use Faster RCNN to detect vehicles under different lighting conditions such as sunny, light, medium and heavy fog conditions. The model's recall is 91.55% for sunny weather and ranges from 72.54 to 57.75% for light, heavy fog conditions. The paper tries to support the use of deep learning models such as Faster RCNN as sufficient evidence so that it could be used in real-time for vehicle detection in foggy conditions and extend the use to pedestrian detection.

2.5 Object Detection in Construction environments

The research (Nath & Behzadan, 2020) tries to evaluate the variants of Yolo namely YOLO-v2 and Yolo to benchmark the performance. A dataset named pictor-v2 is created by gathering 3500 images and 11500 instances having various construction sites under different lighting conditions. The image contains objects of interest such as buildings, equipments and workers. The authors choose transfer learning for both YOLO-v2 and YOLO-v3 models. The models are tested under various categories of datasets. The first category is crowdsourced data with 1105 images, the second category is web-mined consisting of 1402 and the third category is a combination of both the first and second categories. It is observed that YOLO-v3 performs better than YOLO-v2 for small objects and objects that are hard to detect. Also, the YOLO-v3 model, when trained with a combination of crowdsourced data and web-mined data outperformed the older model with an mAP 78.2% on crowdsourced data. On performing sensitivity analysis, it is also observed that the best model predicts more accurately for images that are taken in less crowded scenarios and having better lighting conditions. Additionally, it is concluded that YOLO-v3 is better than YOLO-v2 in detecting construction related objects under different lighting conditions.

2.6 Object Detection for domestic and Military Surveillance

The research (Sarin et al., 2019) tries to solve the challenge of object detection in the context of surveillance in security and military domain to monitor activities in sensitive borders between two or more countries. It outlines the problems of the inability to precisely identify and localize moving objects such as animals, humans under different low-light conditions such as fog, haze and dark conditions. As it is also focused on surveillance, it tries to solve the problem to precisely detect the human body and face. The paper proposes a CNN based approach of combining human, face detection networks and blurred image sensing techniques to distinguish between different types of animals and human activity in poor lighting conditions. It also claims to improve the accuracy of Human and face detection significantly. The advantage of the solution is the use of face detection when the human body is not visible or concealed due to background noise or bad contrast. Another important aspect of the solution is not to use square shaped images of humans rather use images where width is shorter than the height. They also enhance the brightness of the images using the zero centred method. A network similar to ALEX net with a smaller number of filters and a lesser number of fully connected nodes is used. The network is observed to perform well when histogram equalization is performed. The novel approach is combined with models such as HR-ER(Hu & Ramanan, 2017), SSD and S3FD(S. Zhang et al., 2017) independently and tested with publicly available datasets such as DNHD-DB1(Dongguk university, n.d.) CVC-14(Elektra, n.d.) and KAIST(Hwang et al., 2015). it is also tested with face datasets such as Caltech(CALTECH, n.d.), UMIST(Graham & Allinson, n.d.), UFDD(Nada et al., 2018) and Exarch dataset. The authors conclude that the proposed approach, when combined with the HR-ER model, produced the best True Positive Rate(TPR) ranging between 96.3 to 96.83%; however, while combining with SSD, the TPR ranged between 91.49 to 92.8% and combining the approach with S3FD produced the TPR 93.77 to 94.21%.

2.7 Other Novel Approaches for Object detection

The paper(X. Wang et al., 2017) tries to solve the challenge of occlusion and deformation in an object detection scenario. they use an adversarial learning technique so that the network can learn from the generated examples they use this generation-based approach as they argue that all the possible rare scenario of occlusion and deformation cannot be obtained easily in the real world. The idea of their approach is to use an adversarial network to generate all rare occlusion and deformation scenarios so that the object detector can learn from these examples for improved detection during such occlusion and deformation scenarios. In their approach, the learning is a joint exercise between the adversarial network and the actual object detector. As object detectors performance improves, the adversarial network improves the example generation capability, as compared to generating all the examples of occlusion and deformation. The approach generates only hard to learn examples, thus saving training time by only learning from rare scenarios which are difficult to detect. In their experiment, they use a combination of the adversarial network with Fast-RCNN. The tests for performance are conducted on VOC2007 and VOC2012 datasets. It is observed that the new approach improved the mAP by 2.3% and 2.6% on the respective datasets compared to the Fast-RCNN tested with these datasets.

The authors(C.-E. Wu et al., 2019) propose training the neural network with different types of sample images with various lighting. They also remove similar samples. They also maintain a separate sample for day and night for validation. Their idea is to use a light weight detection model so that it can be used with the Nvidia Jetson TX2 device. Therefore ResNet-18(He et al., 2016) Feature pyramid network (FPN) is used for feature extraction along with Cascade RCNN(Cai & Vasconcelos, 2018) so that objects can be detected from different scales and orientations. The input image size for best results used is 960x540.The mAP is 0.53 with a frame rate of 2.3 FPS compared to using ResNet-101(Z. Wu et al., 2019) as FPN, the mAP was 0.60 with a very poor frame rate of 0.17 frames per second. The storage size of the model was also reduced significantly to 57MB by using ResNet-18 FPN with cascade R-CNN.

The paper(Michaelis et al., 2019) tries to study the impact of image distortions, the quality degrades or different weather conditions on object detection performance. The study shows that these problems can bring down the performance of the object detect models by 30-60%. The authors suggest that few data augmentation techniques can improve the performance and robustness of the object detection models significantly. To validate the approach, the augmentation techniques are benchmarked against three popular datasets Pascal-C, Coco-C, Cityscapes-C. These datasets have a variety of image distortions, the quality degrades, and images captured under different weather and lighting conditions also termed as corruption in the context of the paper. The validation is also performed using different variants of RCNN such as Fast RCNN, Faster RCNN, Mask RCNN, Retinanet, Cascade RCNN and Cascade Mask RCNN and Hybrid Task Cascade RNN. Experimental results clearly show that different corruption types in the dataset affect the performance of the model significantly. The robustness of the model depends on the powerfulness of the backbone network. A combination of clean and corrupt data, also known as stylized augmentation, helps improve the robustness of the models. Stylized augmentation also improved the detection performance of the models by about 16% for the PASCAL VOC dataset, 12% for ms-COCO dataset and 41% for Cityscapes. This is achieved, however, with nominal loss of clean data of approximately 2% with each dataset. A key advantage of the augmentation approach is that it can be applied to any image dataset easily.

(Chen et al., 2020) uses a deep learning model for image correction contrast adjustments and noise removal known as visibility complementation module. The processed output is passed to the Yolo network for vehicle detection. The combined architecture is trained for a combination of different types of videos containing glare, hazy and rainy environments. The performance of detection is verified to be improved by 5% and the performance of detection in a rainy condition by 50%. The research further emphasizes the need for improvements and techniques to deal with more hazy and complex conditions.

The work by (Sasagawa & Nagahara, 2020) tries to solve the problem of acquiring datasets of low light that are scarce using generative models. It combines multiple pre-trained models from different domains without needing to train for a specific dataset. The research uses models that are pretrained on pascal voc and COCO datasets. A method of knowledge distillation from pre-trained model is used to build the generative model. The model created is known as YOLO in the dark model. This model is a combination of YOLO and Learn-to-See-in-the-Dark model. which can detect low light images. The approach does not need annotation and training. However, the technique helps to selectively train the layer of the combined model with existing datasets and saves a large amount of training time. It is observed that the generative model has sensitivity 2.4 times better than the YOLO model. However, the encoding speed of the learn-to-see-in-the-Dark is computationally expensive.

In the recent past, there have also been attempts to understand factors that influence object detection (Xiao et al., 2020) try to understand the use of balanced dataset and model creation and parameter initialization and its influence on object detection. They identify reasons for poor object detection as low brightness and contrast, presence of dark areas and noise. They also suggest that improving hardware such as the use of infrared monitoring and increasing the aperture of the camera only increases the cost of the solution. Further, a key finding is that image enhancement as preprocessing step does not help improve the object detection performance. They also try to explain the reason by trying to understand the reason by visualizing the impact of low light on feature preservations in the convolution layers of the network. The authors propose the concept of night vision detector.

They use RFB-Net(S. Liu & Huang, 2018) with a feature pyramid and a context fusion network to detect objects at low light conditions. to create a balanced dataset, they use a publicly available dataset known as ExDARK(Loh & Chan, 2019) and the standard COCO data set which contains images with normal lighting conditions. The approach improved the detection performance by 0.5 per cent to 2.8% when compared to using standard COCO dataset images for low light conditions. They also observe that even after having a balanced dataset with normal and low light images, the model baises towards low light features however this can be corrected by fine tuning the model parameters. It also concludes that lighting conditions play a major role in learning the features for object detection under low light conditions.

Another approach by (K. Wang & Liu, 2020) generates high resolution day images from set of night and day image pairs as input using Game training a deep convolution GAN (DCGAN)(Radford et al., 2015) model. The model is combined with a FASTER RCNN model using convolution-based feature fusion and pooling of multi scale ROI. An important step used in the approach is to use a feature reconstruction mechanism instead of image enhancement methods. Here the training of the model is done in two parts mainly training of DCGAN and the Faster-RCNN model. the GAN model is trained using night-time dataset to get a corresponding data time dataset In the GAN model the discriminator updates the parameter once every two times the generator is trained. The generated image is validated against the daytime dataset by the discriminator to eliminate the instability in the model. Batch normalization is only applied to the output layer of the generator. It is also applied to the input layer of the discriminator. Once the generator is stabilized the weights are not changed, and the GAN model output is synced to train the Faster-RCNN. Different hyper parameters are tuned, and dropouts are used to avoid overfitting. ImageNet pretrained VGG-16(Simonyan & Zisserman, 2015) model is used as Region Proposal Network for feature extraction; additionally, multi scale feature fusion and pooling technique is also used. The experiments conducted show that the new approach achieves an mAP of 82.6% for night images as compared to 80.4% with traditional Faster-RCNN.

The approach proposed by(H. H. C. Nguyen et al., 2020) recommend the use of an image enhancement neural network. The image enhances neural network learns from a large amount of noisy images. It outputs the enhanced image by removing certain distortions. These images are then normalized and rasterized to get the enhanced images. These enhanced images are passed to Faster RCNN trained using the saliency map of the dataset. Saliency map is a mechanism to identify the unique feature of the image. The bounding boxes are generated on the saliency maps of the distorted image. The Faster RCNN network finally outputs the bounding box on the actual distorted image for all the objects that are not clearly visible.

The paper(Junhao Wang, 2021) tries to solve the problem to have a single object detection model for both night-time and daytime under various lighting conditions such as earthquakes, landslides and floods. The author proposes improvising yolov3 object detection model by combining it with the Retinex model, which is good at enhancement of the images with poor lighting conditions. the experiments conducted reveal the model's average precision improved in a range between 53.23 - 59.79% when tested under different poor visibility conditions when compared to the standalone YoloV3 model.

2.8 Summary

After analysing several approaches on low light object detection in the past, we see there is yet a lot to be explored in the domain. The key challenges include the availability of datasets with low and poor lighting conditions. Some of the proposed approaches demand a large amount of training time very complex compute intensive neural network architecture to solve the problem. Notionally some state of art methods conclude that image enhancement methods do not help in low light object detection tasks. Further, some of the past studies conclude trained models on normal lighting conditions do not help with low light object detection. However this finding needs further analysis. In this research work, our idea is not to disagree with state-of-the-art approaches but to enrich and complement existing approaches.

The focus in this study is use of pretrained models or find a minimalistic training approach. Additionally, we try to understand image processing techniques such denoising and image enhancement techniques with an objective to improve object detection performance and speed. Our idea is also to understand and analyse the approaches from the past with a new perceptive to improve object detection performance and speed of low light images. In summary, we would like to build a simplified and intuitive approach with a focus on image processing techniques that may include denoising image enhancement and use of pretrained models and minimalistic training approaches.

Chapter 3   RESEARCH METHODOLOGY

3.1   Introduction.

This chapter outlines our approach to solve the problem of low light object detection. It also explains the changes and modifications in the original research methodology mentioned in the research proposal phase. The changes are brought into the methodology after gaining valuable insights from the literature survey of the state of art methods applied. We also foresee tremendous research opportunities using image enhancement and pretrained models to improvise existing deep learning-based object detection methods.

3.2   Our Approach

The flow chart in figure 3.1 depicts the steps of our methodology; this includes loading and understanding various image datasets, choosing a set of low light images by manual inspection of various datasets considered under the study. The images are annotated to identify the ground truth of reference. These images are further subjected to preprocessing steps, such as resizing the image to standard size and orientation. The next step is applying image enhancement to improve contrast and illumination. The research would then proceed to use at least three pretrained object detection models and experiment the object detection performance by subjecting the images to different image enhancement methods. The speed of detection is also recorded. The study's findings such as benefit gains or drawbacks and the lessons learnt are summarized to conclude the research study. The details of some important steps and the rationale behind the choice of models and the explanation of denoising and Image enhancement which are probable candidates of the experiment in our approach are described in sections 3.3 to 3.6

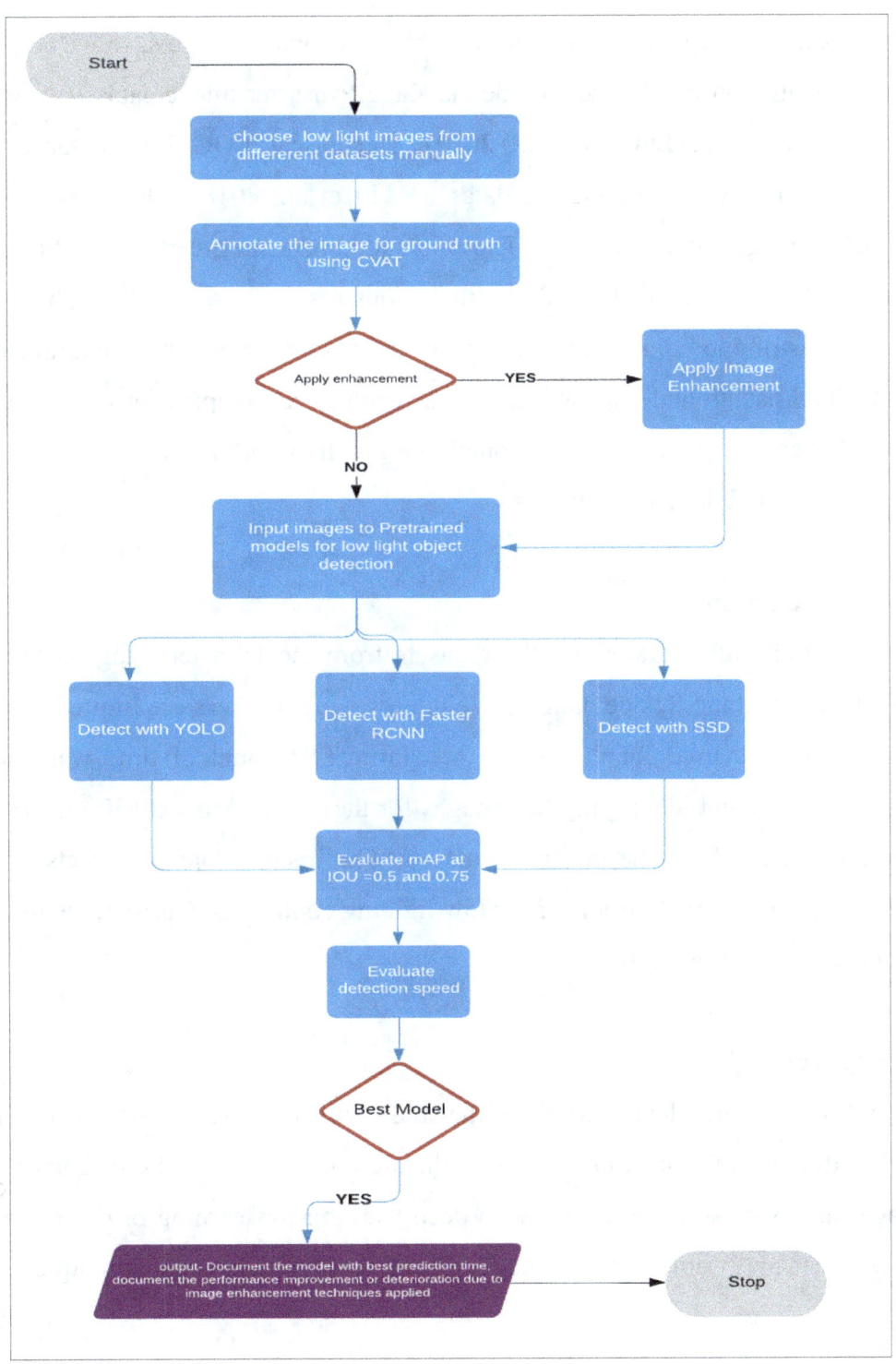

Figure 3.1 Flow chart of our Research methodology for low light object detection

3.3 Dataset Description

The low light bad weather datasets are not available as standard datasets, so we collect these from various online image sources. These include the Kaggle disaster image dataset(yelon, 2020), low-light images from GitHub(Ethan-Weber, 2020), The Pascal VOC 2008 dataset (Pascal-VOC, 2008), low-light images and the Reside dataset(B. Li et al., 2018). The disaster image dataset consists of 4500 images of 4 categories. These include hurricanes, earthquake floods and Forest-fire. These are RGB images with 96 dpi with various resolutions. The GitHub low light image repository consists of 4 low light and bad weather images captured during natural calamities. The Pascal VOC 2008 has around 70 low light images, which are helpful for our study. Finally, the Reside dataset is an extensive collection containing low light, hazy images of types synthetic and real for both indoor and outdoor scenarios.

3.4 Dataset Selection

As part of the study, after examining the datasets from the Disaster image dataset, the Pascal VOC 2008 dataset and the Reside dataset. We understood that there are limited low light images so that these could be used for the study. A significant amount of time was spent manually inspecting the images and identifying the images for the study. Around 150 images were chosen for our experiment out from the different datasets. The images contain objects such as people, animals, vehicles, planes, pedestrians under low lighting conditions. Current, the low light images are determined by visual inspection.

3.5 Pre-processing

The low light bad weather dataset used for the study will be subject to preprocessing steps such as converting to uniform size denoising, normalization and adjusting the brightness and contrast of the images are made suitable for use with deep learning for learning or detection purposes. In our study we try to apply at least three image enhancement or denoising techniques.

3.5.1 Denoising

Denoising is a set of techniques in digital image processing used to remove noise from an image. In our approach, we may consider either of the following technique namely Median Filter, Non-

Local Mean Filter a Laplacian Filter. The detailed explanation of each technique is explained in sections 3.5.1.1 to 3.5.1.3

3.5.1.1 Median Filter

Median filter(Arce, 2005) is a special type of filter which replaces the pixel with the median value from a sample of chosen window size in the region of interest in the image the median filter size is usually odd for example, 3x3 5x5 7x7 and so on it is a nonlinear filter used to remove salt and pepper noise it is a very important filter in image processing as it preserves the edges. The median filter is expressed mathematically as

$$f(x,y) = \text{median}_{(s,t) \in S_{x,y}} \{g(s,t)\}$$

Figure 3.2 Equation for median filter

g(s,t) is a function that represents the intensity value of the pixel for the kernel coordinates s,t from the actual image .f(x,y) represents the median filtering function

3.5.1.2 Non-Local Mean Filter

Nonlocal mean(Buades et al., 2011) is a special type of filter which replaces the target pixel using weighted average of the pixel values in the whole image. The weight of each pixel value used is based on the similarity of the pixels with the target pixel chosen for replacement. The method is more effective than the median filter in removing salt and pepper noise; however, the method is computationally expensive. The non-local mean filter is mathematically represented as

$$g(p) = \frac{1}{Z} \sum_{q \in I} B_w(p-q) G_\sigma(N_p - N_q) f(q)$$

$$G_\sigma(x) = e^{-\left(\frac{\sum_i x_i^2}{2\sigma^2}\right)}$$

$$Z = \sum_{q \in I} B_w(p-q) G_\sigma(N_p - N_q)$$

$$B_w = \begin{cases} 1, & if\ max(|x_1|,|x_2|)\ x \leq W \\ 0, & otherwise \end{cases}$$

Figure 3.3 Equations for Non-Local Mean Filter

The function g(p) represents the Nonlocal mean filter, Gσ(x) represents gaussian weights based on different intensities. Z is used as Normalization function Bw is a neighbourhood search function, and the weights purely depend on the neighbourhood similarity difference represented by 2 pixels p and q

3.5.1.3   Laplacian filter

The Laplacian filter is used to identify the quick change in the illuminated areas of the image. It is also used to identify the edges in the image. One advantage of this technique is that it can be used to remove speckle noise from the image when combined with a Gaussian filter. The Laplacian value of the pixel is calculated using the weighted average of the pixel values around it. Since the method uses a second order derivative to calculate the pixel value, it is highly sensitive to noise. It has prerequisite to run a gaussian filter as a mandatory preprocessing step additionally, the Laplacian filter can implement using one of the two standard kernels widely used for denoising the images. Laplacian filter is second order image improvement method. It is mathematically represented as

$$\nabla^2 I = \frac{\partial^2 I}{\partial x^2} + \frac{\partial^2 I}{\partial y^2}$$

Figure 3.4 Equation for Laplacian Filter

The parameter I represents the Image ∇^2 represents the Laplacian smoothing function for the image.

3.5.2   Image Contrast Adjustment

Image Contrast Adjustment is used to improve the illumination of the image. It is also used to distribute the brightness in the image so that the objects in the darker part of the image is improved. As part of the Image enhancement step in our approach, we would consider either of the following technique that include Gama Based Correction, Log Based Correction, Histogram Equalization and Contrast stretching methods. The detailed explanation of each of the techniques is explained in sections 3.5.2.1 to 3.5.2.5

3.5.2.1 Gamma Based Correction

Gamma Correction(Solomon & Breckon, 2011) is a method that uses power transform on the image pixel values to correct the illumination setting of the image. If the value of gamma correction is less than 1, the image gets darker and if it is greater than 1, the image gets brighter. This is a standard image illumination correction mechanism provided in monitors, cell phone screens and digital cameras as images are acquired at different lighting conditions.

3.5.2.2 log-based Correction

Log transformation(Solomon & Breckon, 2011) based correction is more aggressive than Gamma correction mechanism as it stretches the illumination of the pixels. The approach should only be used when there are too many dark pixels in the images in other scenarios; the correction would lead to the loss of information from the image.

3.5.2.3 Histogram Equalization

Histogram Equalization(Solomon & Breckon, 2011) is an image processing method that corrects the contrast of the image by using its histogram of intensities and frequencies. The histogram of the image is created by plotting the intensities on the x-axis and frequency on the y axis. Histogram equalization distributes or stretches the pixel intensity in such a way that regions having very low or no intensity are also illuminated so that they can be identified easily.

3.5.2.4 Contrast limited Histogram Equalization (CLAHE)

CLAHE is a histogram-based equalization technique which tries to avoid over amplification of brightness when compared to Histogram equalization, which uses global contrast. This method works on small areas known as regions and equalizes these areas. the neighbouring regions are combined using bilinear interpolation to complete the enhancement process and to remove artificial region boundaries .one advantage of this technique is that it does not overamplify areas with uniform brightness

3.5.2.5 Minmax Contrast Stretching

Min-Max contrast stretching is an image enhancement technique where the minimum and maximum values of the pixels in the image are stretched to use the complete range of brightness values as a result the pixel brightness values are stretched to use a new range. This is also known as image normalization. This is a linear technique due to which the original image can be obtained back using a linear transformation. This is one of the standard digital image enhancement techniques built into imaging systems.

3.6 Use of Pretrained Models

A set of pretrained general-purpose object detection models will be used to understand the detection performance and speed in the context of the low light images with the images chosen from the datasets used in this research. As we have chosen to use atleast three pretrained model which include Faster RCNN, Yolo and SSD

3.7 Choice of pretrained models for the study

3.7.1 Yolo.

Yolo variants use Regression as their core idea to solve the object detection problem. They use a Single CNN to predict the bounding boxes and probabilities of the object classes associated with the box simultaneously. It does not process the image in parts instead uses the whole image during its training and testing phase. The model is of particular interest for the study due to its simplicity in the architecture and speed of detection .it also understands the features in a generic way and does not have problems with background scenes.

3.7.2 SSD

SSD uses small convolution filters and a small set of default boxes .it also uses feature maps of different scales to detect objects for different aspect ratios. Additionally, the model uses a novel loss function. The loss function is the weighted sum of localisation and confidence loss. The model is important for our study as it can detect objects in images of very low resolution. It also provides a good balance between accuracy and speed of detection.

3.7.3 Fast RCNN

Fast RCNN uses an image and a set of region proposals as input. It uses convolution and pooling to generate the feature map. It also uses a technique called ROI pooling for extracting the features from the feature map. The ROI pooling layer is used to extract small feature maps of fixed spatial dimensions from the areas of the valid region of interest. These features are then processed by a set of fully connected layers to two provide two outputs. The first output provides the probability of each class of the object being identified. The second output contains four values corresponding to the position of the bounding box for each object class identified. The network also uses SoftMax instead of SVM for classification. The network is of significance in the study as it uses the image directly as input and Idea of Convolution to restrict the number of selective searches to one per image. It has better quality object detection capabilities and uses less disk space when compared to RCNN.

3.7.4 The Faster RCNN

It contains two parts. The first one is Convolution Neural Network that creates region proposal also known as the RPN Region Proposal Network. The RPN takes images of varied sizes and outputs region proposals and a confidence score. The Second part is Fast RCNN which uses the region proposal to predict objects. The model uses translation-invariant anchors and a pyramid of filters. The computations are also shared between the network, making it faster than the Fast R-CNN. This model is important for our study as it helps detect objects in different orientations or translation conditions with good accuracy.

3.8 Metric and evaluation of the new approach

As the first step, we would construct a ground truth table for the chosen images used for the study. Various image enhancement techniques will be applied to the chosen images and passed as input to the pretrained models chosen for the study. The model's inference outcome will be evaluated for metrics such as mAP and IOU, and the detection speed is measured in milli seconds. Finally, the performance and speed of the chosen three object detection model when subjected to different enhancement techniques is measured.

3.9 Summary

The methodology explained in the chapter for low light object detection is evolving. We are trying to understand different ways of identifying low light images as it has been done by manually inspecting images from multiple datasets, which seems to be one of the most challenging limitations of the approach. We have also tried to understand different denoising and image enhancement techniques.

After our interim submission, we further refined our methodology to explore and restrict our study to a few image enhancement techniques such as Gamma Correction, Histogram equalization and Minmax Contrast Stretching. We also modified our research methodology flow chart accordingly. The pretrained models identified are Faster RCNN, YOLO and SSD. we conduct experiments to validate our methodology both in terms of detection performance and speed of detection. The details are provided in the following chapters. It is also our constant effort to focus on minimalistic training such as using pretrained models and processing the low light image by better understanding the image enhancement techniques which are also key contributors of our methodology.

Chapter 4   IMPLEMENTATION AND ANALYSIS

4.1   Introduction

In this chapter, we explain the granular details on the implementation of low light object detection using pretrained models and image enhancement techniques. We start the implementation with low light image identification from three datasets to create a custom dataset of lowlight images. This is followed by identifying object classes of interest and providing details on how we perform annotation and ground truth preparation. We also provide some snapshots of the distribution of the object classes of interest. We explain different tools and libraries used to create and process the ground truth. The chapter further elaborates different other steps, such as the need of resizing the images followed by choice and details of pretrained models and the weights. We also further provide the details of the experimental setup, the details of a number of experimental scenarios for our study, the parameters used are explained. Some details on the libraries and functions used to implement image enhancement techniques are also explained. In the final parts of the chapter, we highlight details of the implementation of metrics used for measuring the model performance and the speed of object detection

4.2   Data Preparation and Preprocessing

As part of the data preparation and preprocessing, we perform the following steps in sequence: low light image identification and custom dataset creation. This is followed by image resizing. We further identify the object classes of interest and then annotate the images. We also further process the ground truth so that it can be used as a reference in our experiment. Each of these steps are explained in detail in sections 4.2.1 to 4.2.6

4.2.1   Low light Image Identification

This is a manual step where we use three datasets, namely Reside outdoor dataset, Disaster management dataset and Pascal VOC dataset. We manually inspected each image carefully in two iterations to identify close to 155 images from these datasets and created a custom dataset with 125 low light images. The images used in our research are mostly RGB and uses jpeg format. As the process of identification of low light images was manual, it consumed a significant amount of time during our research

4.2.2 Image Resizing

In this step, we resize the identified lowlight images to a standard dimension of 500x500. We achieve this using the python OpenCV(opencv.org, n.d.) image resize function to automate the resizing task. After resizing the images, they are stored in a separate folder so that the original images are not overwritten.

4.2.3 Image Annotation

We use CVAT(cvat.org, 2020) an open-source tool from intel for image annotation or labelling of object classes. The tool helps to label the object classes manually using different types of bounding boxes such as rectangular and polygon. In this study, we use rectangular bounding boxes for annotation. After annotating the images, the tool also helps us to export the annotations to COCO (cocodataset.org, n.d.)format. The annotation export structure contains two folders, namely images and annotations. The images folder contains all the images that were annotated, and the annotations folder contains a JSON file containing the ground truth bounding box annotations for each image. The tool provides other annotation formats as well however for this study we export the dataset to COCO 1.0 annotation format.

4.2.4 Description of classes for low light object detection

In this study, we consider a subset of object classes that are of interest in the coco dataset. We try to use these classes in the context of our dataset with 125 lowlight images. These include fourteen classes namely car, person, airplane, bus, truck, cat, dog, street sign, bird, boat, bicycle, horse, train, motorcycle.

4.2.5 Ground Truth Processing

In our study, we used pycoco, a python library to process the ground truth stored in the coco format. The library provides easy high-level functions to convert the JSON in coco format to a table (pandas data frame), as shown in Fig 4.1. The imported ground truth details of the bounding boxes from the images can be used conveniently for further processing and comparison.

	image_id	area	id	category	col_left	row_top	width	height	iscrowd	img_file_name	img_width	img_height
0	1	17437.6432	1	Car	265.81	351.72	140.99	123.68	0	0058_0.9_0.04.jpg	500	500
1	1	7779.4080	2	Car	0.00	370.98	95.90	81.12	0	0058_0.9_0.04.jpg	500	500
2	1	2366.4576	3	Car	124.83	387.20	64.87	36.48	0	0058_0.9_0.04.jpg	500	500
3	1	3532.1652	4	Car	87.54	378.07	58.84	60.03	0	0058_0.9_0.04.jpg	500	500
4	1	1014.4220	5	person	218.70	376.55	27.80	36.49	0	0058_0.9_0.04.jpg	500	500
...	...	...	...	...	...	...	...	...	...	...	...	...
518	140	3444.8010	519	street sign	320.00	182.91	39.19	87.90	0	flood_539.jpg	500	500
519	140	1800.1614	520	Car	261.36	201.81	37.34	48.21	0	flood_539.jpg	500	500
520	141	17060.1200	521	bicycle	306.73	280.27	178.64	95.50	0	flood_549.jpg	500	500
521	141	20380.2195	522	person	360.13	130.92	112.01	181.95	0	flood_549.jpg	500	500
522	142	8033.7408	523	person	221.66	215.05	46.32	173.44	0	wf_person.jpg	500	500

Figure 4.1 Ground truth Annotations converted to a Data frame

4.2.6 Distribution of Classes in the dataset

The distribution of fourteen object classes across 125 low light images in the dataset is depicted in figure 4.2. The dataset contains person and car as important object classes. It is observed that the dataset has imbalanced object classes.

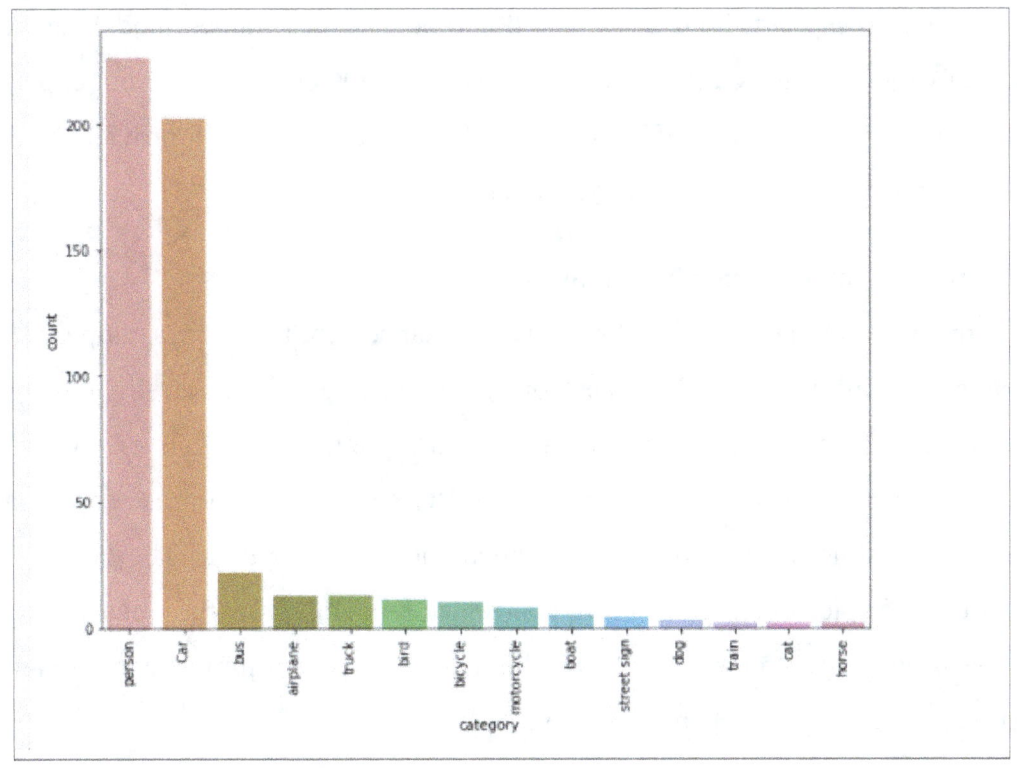

Figure 4.2 Distribution of object class in 125 low light images

4.3 Selection of Pretrained Models and weights

In our study, we used three pretrained models, namely Faster RCNN, YOLO and SSD. This is in line with the steps defined in our research methodology section. We used GluonCV and mxnet neural network libraries for our experiment implementation. This was the preferred choice since the Gluon model zoo provides all the three models in a single framework. Additionally, it provides high level functions to load the models and their weights easily.

Table 4.1 Pretrained models and their weights and presets

Model	Pretrained weights	Weight names -gluon convention	Other Presets
Faster RCNN	MS COCO	faster_rcnn_fpn_resnet50_v1b_coco	Image size -500x500
YOLO	MS COCO	yolo3_darknet53_coco	Image size -500x500
SSD	MS COCO	ssd_512_resnet50_v1_coco	Image size -500x500

The library also supports both CPU and GPU mode. The pretrained model zoo also provides the option of various weights. In our scenario, we chose COCO weights for our experiments with low light images and used the CPU version of the library. Table 4.1 provides a detailed view of models and weight choices for our experiment

4.4 Image Enhancement Techniques

In our research, we have applied three image enhancement techniques, namely Gama correction, Histogram equalization and Minmax contrast stretching to our low light images and tried to understand their effect on the performance of the pretrained models of interest independently. These enhancement techniques are applied on RGB images. In the case of Gama correction, we have used existing state of the art implementation using python. The Histogram equalization technique is implemented by using equalizehist function from the open cv library. Similarly, contrast stretching is implemented with the help of a custom implementation and the normalize function provided by the OpenCV library.

Since we try to understand the effect of enhancement techniques independently, the low light images are subjected to these enhancement techniques and stored in separate folders with the folder name associated with the corresponding enhancement technique. This approach is chosen due to several important reasons, firstly to avoid the need for changing the names of images themselves. Another objective to maintain the original name of the image is to facilitate comparison of the prediction performance of the model with Ground truth. In the comparison step, we use image names as a standard reference to compare the resultant bounding boxes with actual ground truth bounding boxes. Finally, the folder-based approach helps in maintaining the original images and the enhanced images in a systematic way without having to replace and original image after enhancement.

4.5 Experimental infrastructure Setup

We used Ubuntu 18.04 LTS 64-bit edition running on an Intel i7 processor and 32 GB of RAM. We used Jupyter notebook with Anaconda python environment. The libraries used include pycoco for annotation parsing, GluonCV zoo for pretrained model loading and object detection bounding box prediction. Matplotlib and seaborn for visualization and analysis. Pyodi for interconverting bounding box format. We also used OpenCV and skimage for preprocessing and image enhancement. We also reused the mAP calculation implementation from map-boxes metric API.

4.6 Experimental Scenarios

We conducted 24 experiments with our low light image dataset with three pretrained neural network models both with and without applying image enhancement techniques. The table 4.2 describes the details of each experiment and their settings in detail. The results of the experiments and their analysis will be elaborated in chapter 5.

Table 4.2 Details of the experiments and their configurations

Experiment details	Model	Enhancement type	parameters	IOU threshold
Faster-RCNN without enhancement	Faster RCNN	None		0.5
Yolo without enhancement	YOLO	None		0.5
SSD without enhancement	SSD	None		0.5
Faster-RCNN with Gama Correction	Faster RCNN	Gama correction	Gama=1.50	0.5
Yolo with Gama Correction	YOLO	Gama correction	Gama=1.50	0.5

SSD with Gama Correction	SSD	Gama correction	Gama=1.50	0.5
Faster-RCNN with histogram equalization	Faster RCNN	Histogram equalization		0.5
Yolo with histogram equalization	YOLO	Histogram equalization		0.5
SSD with histogram equalization	SSD	Histogram equalization		0.5
Faster-RCNN with min-max contrast stretching	Faster RCNN	Contrast stretching	alpha=0 beta=0.8	0.5
Yolo with min-max contrast stretching	YOLO	Contrast stretching	alpha=0 beta=0.8	0.5
SSD with min-max contrast stretching	SSD	Contrast stretching	alpha=0 beta=0.8	0.5
Faster-RCNN without enhancement	Faster RCNN	None		0.75
Yolo without enhancement	YOLO	None		0.75
SSD without enhancement	SSD	None		0.75
Faster-RCNN with Gama Correction	Faster RCNN	Gamma correction	Gama=1.50	0.75
Yolo with Gama Correction	YOLO	Gamma correction	Gama=1.50	0.75
SSD with Gama Correction	SSD	Gama correction	Gama=1.50	0.75
Faster-RCNN with histogram equalization	Faster RCNN	Histogram equalization		0.75
Yolo with histogram equalization	YOLO	Histogram equalization		0.75
SSD with histogram equalization	SSD	Histogram equalization		0.75
Faster-RCNN with min-max contrast stretching	Faster RCNN	Contrast stretching	alpha=0 beta=0.8	0.75
Yolo with min-max contrast stretching	YOLO	Contrast stretching	alpha=0	0.75

			beta=0.8	
SSD with min-max contrast stretching	SSD	Contrast stretching	alpha=0 beta=0.8	0.75

4.7 Measurement of Model Performance and Speed of Inference

We use three important metrics for measuring the model's performance, namely confidence score, mAP and IOU threshold. We use prediction time in milliseconds to understand the low light object detection models inference speed for different scenarios as described in table 4.2

4.7.1 Confidence Score

In our study. The confidence score helps us determine the possibility of an object being present in the bounding boxes inferred by the object detection model. Its value ranges between 0 and 1 a score of 0 indicates that the desired object of interest is not present in the bounding box and a score of 1 indicates that the object of interest is highly likely to be present in the bounding box predicted by the model

4.7.2 Intersection Over Union (IOU)

We also use the IOU threshold as part of our study. It is also known as Jaccard Index. It helps us to determine the degree of overlap between the actual ground truth bounding boxes and the bounding boxes predicted by the object detection model. A value >0.5 is true positive. In our experiment, we evaluate the model performance at two IOU threshold values, namely 0.5 and 0.75

4.7.3 Mean Average Precision (mAP)

In our study, we use mAP as a metric to measure the correctness of Object detection across multiple object classes. To calculate the mAP, we first calculate the average precision of detection of each object class detected by the model at a particular IOU threshold. We calculate the mAP by calculating the mean of the average precision across multiple object classes of interest. The mAP in our scenario was calculated at the IOU threshold values of 0.5 and 0.75

A challenge in our implementation was that the ground truth bounding boxes were in COCO format and the prediction bounding boxes output by our object detection model was in corners format (xmin,ymin,xmax,ymax), so we converted the prediction bounding boxes to corners format from coco format using the bounding box conversion APIs of Pyodi library. We reused the mapBoxes library to calculate the mAP.

4.7.4 Prediction time

As part of our research, we also captured the time taken to detect the object of interest by different object detection models measured in milliseconds for various experimental scenarios.

4.8 Summary

The chapter provides a comprehensive overview of the implementation of the study to understand object detection in lowlight using pretrained models and the use of image enhancement techniques. It explains the difficulty of identifying low light images from three datasets resulting in a lot of time spent in manual identification and annotation .it also explains the tools used for manual annotation, the format of exporting annotation and the libraries used in ground truth processing and the distribution of the object classes of interest. All these steps are explained from sections 4.2.1 through 4.2.6. we choose three models Faster RCNN, YOLO and SSD with pretrained coco weights. The details of the model presets and the library settings are provided in section 4.3. The choice of image enhancement techniques, the organization of images for comparison is covered in section 4.4. The experimental infrastructure setup for the experiment is explained in 4.5. different models and enhancement parameters, and the details of 24 experiments to understand the model performance and prediction speed with different enhancement techniques at IOU threshold 0.5 and 0.75 are elaborated in sections 4.6. Finally, we explain the key metric under the study, namely confidence score, Intersection over Union and mAP in section 4.7.

Chapter 5 RESULTS AND DISCUSSION

5.1 Introduction

In this chapter we present some findings and discuss the results of the 24 experiments that were conducted with three goals in mind, firstly to understand the applicability of pretrained object detection model in the context of low light images. Secondly on whether certain image processing techniques like image enhancement when applied, contribute to the performance of object detection models and speed of detection. The chapter explains how individual results of an experiment are based on the enhancement parameters and the presets used to observe the object detection performance. The final part of our chapter also captures the prediction speeds of the pretrained models when the low light images are subjected to the image enhancement techniques.

5.2 Experiment without Enhancement Scenarios

We conducted experiments with our low light image dataset with three pretrained models, namely Faster RCNN Yolo and SSD without image enhancement for IOU thresholds of 0.50 and 0.75. We use experimental scenarios performed without enhancements as baseline measurements for comparison with enhancement scenarios at corresponding IOU thresholds.

Table 5.1 Baseline experiment for low light images without enhancement at IOU=0.5

Model	Enhancement criteria	parameters	mAP Range		Confidence score	
			Min	Max	Min	Max
Faster RCNN	No Enhancement	IOU=0.5	42.42	71.07	57.71	96.68
YOLO	No Enhancement	IOU=0.5	44.40	71.34	56.85	91.33
SSD	No Enhancement	IOU=0.5	40.89	67.93	54.09	89.85

Table 5.2 Baseline experiment for low light images without enhancement at IOU=0.75

Model	Enhancement criteria	parameters	mAP Range		Confidence score	
			Min	Max	Min	Max
Faster RCNN	No enhancement	IOU=0.75	17	54.63	30.25	97.65
YOLO	No enhancement	IOU=0.75	17.52	49.79	32.37	91.97
SSD	No Enhancement	IOU=0.75	16.76	52.17	31.26	93.77

5.3 Experiment with Enhancement Scenarios

We used three image enhancement techniques to understand the object detection performance in low light conditions. We use COCO weights for all the experiments for our pretrained models. We also captured the low light object detection performance at the same two IOC thresholds that were used for the previous experiments. Sections 5.3.1 to 5.3.3 explain the findings of 24 experiments conducted and the comparison results. As a convention, in the future sections, we always look at the Max values (the best performance values) to compare the model performance in terms of mAP and confidence score. However, we mention the whole range of Min and Max values in the table.

5.3.1 Experiments with Gamma Correction

Gamma correction improves the illumination condition of the low light image. when we applied the enhancement on our low light images, we observed the detection performance of YOLO improved by an additional maP score of ~1.75% and SSD by ~1.25% when compared to baseline measurement at IOU=0.5

Table 5.3 Experiment with low light images with gamma correction at IOU=0.5

Model	Enhancement criteria	parameters	Map Range		Confidence score	
			Min	Max	Min	Max
Faster RCNN	Gama Correction	IOU=0.5 gamma =1.5	43.57	70.58	58.82	95.28
YOLO	Gama Correction	IOU=0.5 gamma =1.5	45.11	73.07	56.25	91.12
SSD	Gama Correction	IOU=0.5 gamma =1.5	43.08	69.21	55.88	89.78

When we made the IOU threshold more stringent to 0.75 and measure the detection performance of YOLO with gamma correction improved by ~4% and SSD by 0.2%

Table 5.4 Experiment with low light images with gamma correction at IOU=0.75

Model	Enhancement criteria	parameters	Map Range		Confidence score	
			Min	Max	Min	Max
Faster RCNN	Gama Correction	IOU=0.75 gamma =1.5	17.56	52.15	32.67	97.04
YOLO	Gama Correction	IOU=0.75 gamma =1.5	18.89	53.67	32.80	93.17
SSD	Gama Correction	IOU=0.75 gamma =1.5	16.23	52.27	29.13	93.61

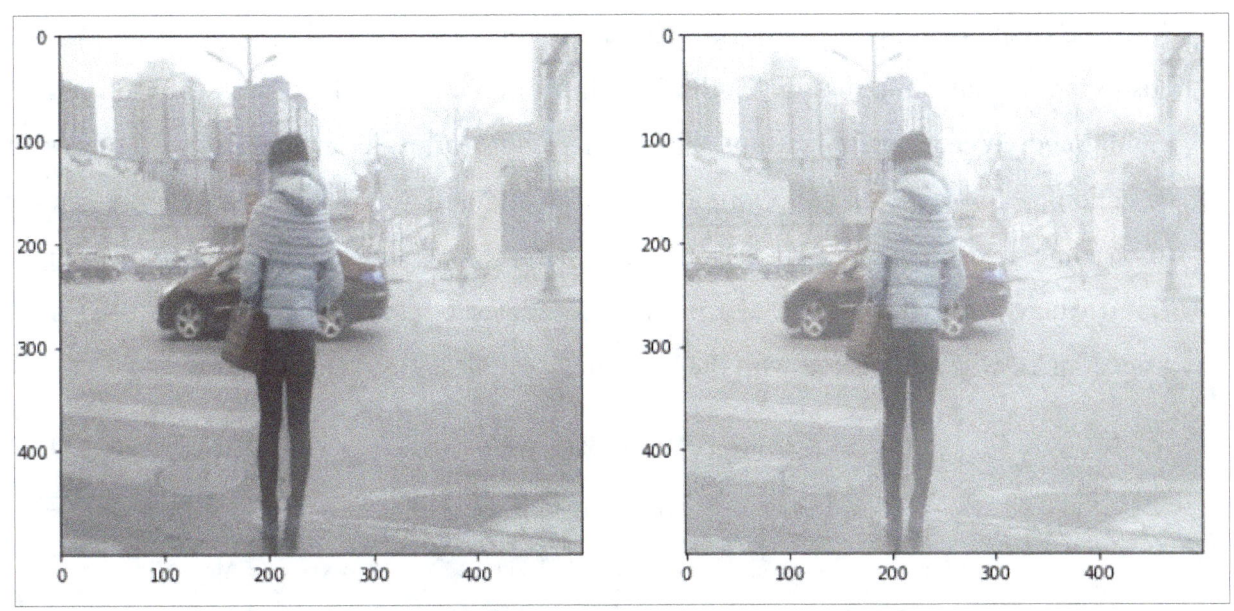

Figure 5.1 Raw image, image with Gamma correction =1.5

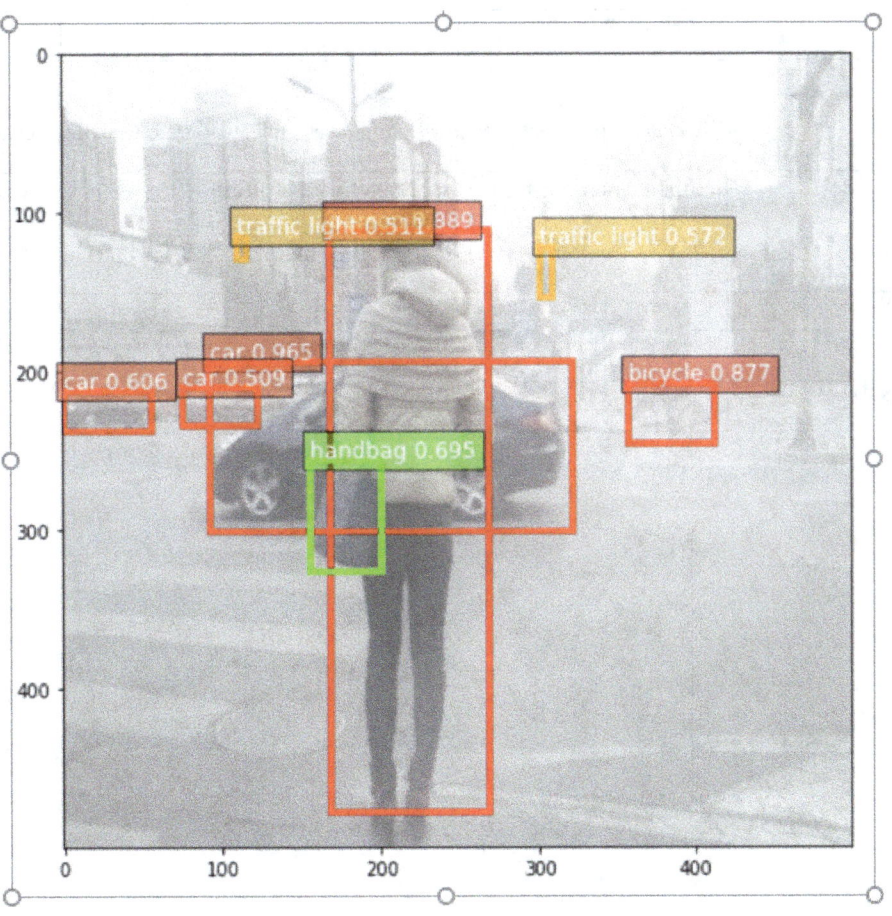

Figure 5.2 Example image with objects detected after Gamma Correction

the confidence score for Yolo improved by 2% and SSD by 3.75%

5.3.2 Experiments with Histogram Equalization

Histogram equalization distributes the illumination, so that lowlight areas of the image also get highlighted. When we applied the enhancement on our low light images, we observed that the detection performance of YOLO improved by an additional maP score of ~2.6% when compared to baseline measurement at IOU=0.5. The Faster RCNN models performance also improved by 2.5%. There was deterioration of model performance by ~1.5% percent with SSD model with respect mAP when compared with the baseline.

Table 5.5 Experiment with low light images with Histogram Equalization at IOU=0.50

Model	Enhancement criteria	parameters	mAP Range		Confidence score	
			Min	Max	Min	Max
Faster RCNN	Histogram equalization	IOU=0.5	43.94	73.60	57.36	96.09
YOLO	Histogram equalization	IOU=0.5	45.27	73.94	56.15	91.72
SSD	Histogram equalization	IOU=0.5	39.24	67.47	52.15	89.67

Table 5.6 Experiment with low light images with Histogram Equalization at IOU=0.75

Model	Enhancement criteria	parameters	Map Range		Confidence score	
			Min	Max	Min	Max
Faster RCNN	Histogram equalization	IOU=0.75	15.55	49.18	31.08	98.25
YOLO	Histogram equalization	IOU=0.75	19.92	54.23	34.23	93.18
SSD	Histogram equalization	IOU=0.75	16.66	65.25	23.80	93.44

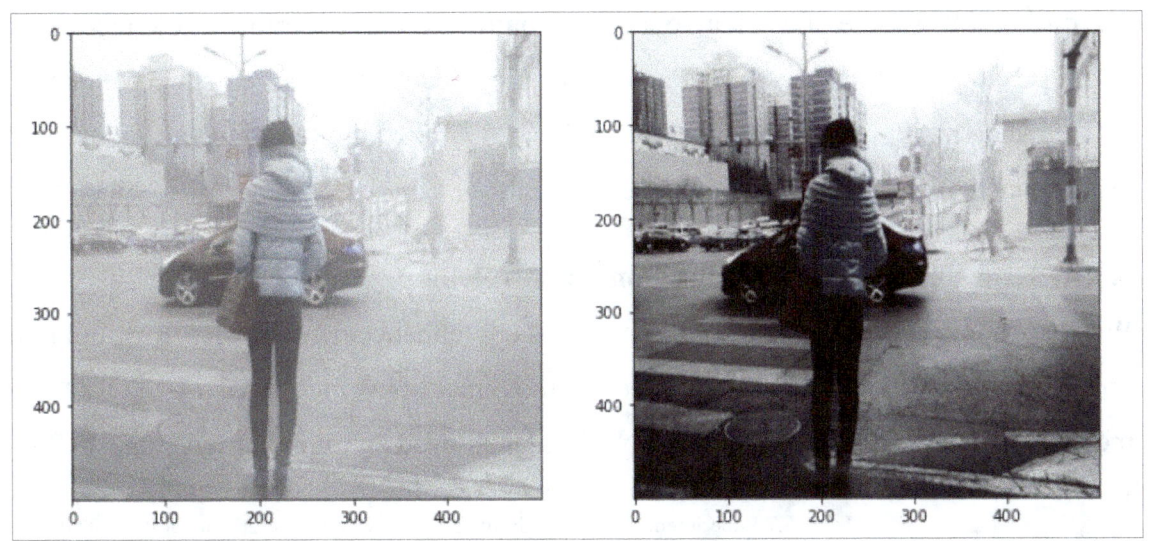

Figure 5.3 Raw image, Histogram equalized image

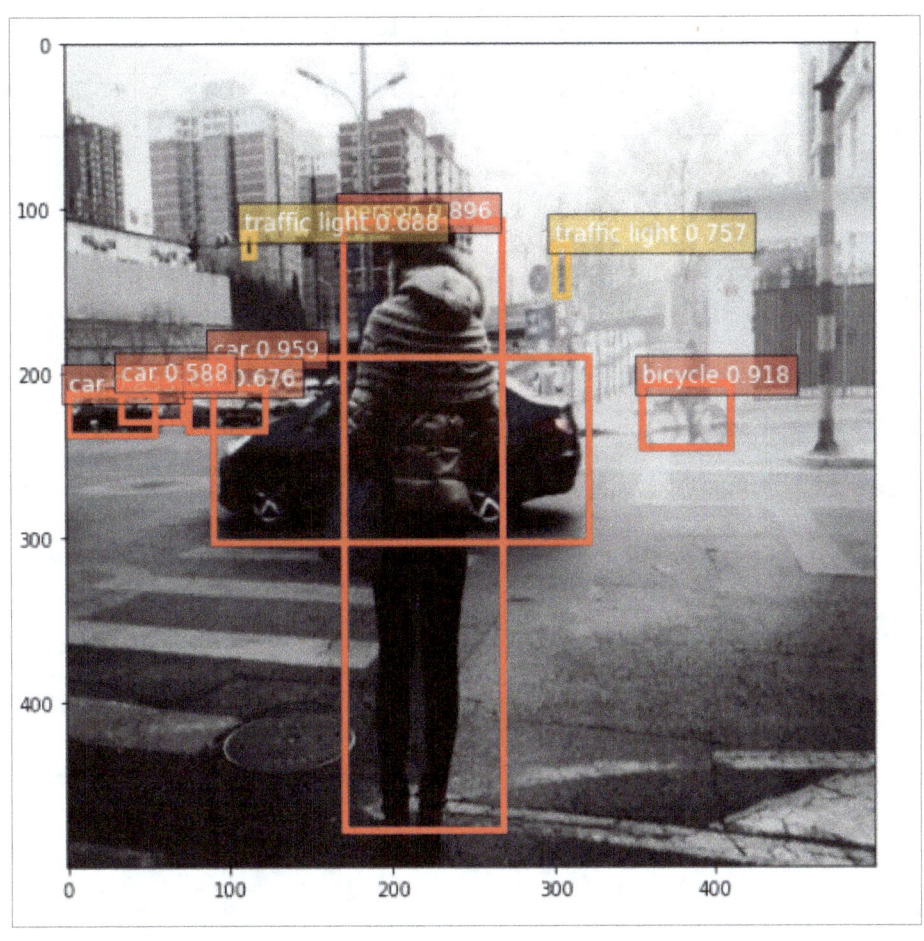

Figure 5.4 Example image with objects detected after Histogram Equalization

To further investigate the behaviour. We continued our experiment by increasing the IOU threshold =0.75 to compare with the corresponding baseline measurements. We observed that the performance(mAP) of YOLO improved by 4.4% and the confidence score of 1.5%. The performance of the SSD model improved by 13.8%

5.3.3 Experiments with Minmax Contrast stretching

We also applied the minmax contrast stretching enhancement on our low light images. We observed very marginal performance improvement in the case of YOLO for baseline measurement at IOU=0.5. The fast RCNN model showed an improvement close to 2%.

Table 5.7 Experiment with low light images with Contrast Stretching at IOU=0.50

Model	Enhancement criteria	parameters	mAP Range		Confidence score	
			Min	Max	Min	Max
Faster RCNN	Minmax contrast stretching	IOU=0.5	43.33	73.21	56.44	95.37
YOLO	Minmax contrast stretching	IOU=0.5	44.80	71.39	57.17	91.10
SSD	Minmax contrast stretching	IOU=0.5	41.94	66.33	56.90	89.94

Table 5.8 Experiment with low light images with Contrast Stretching at IOU=0.75

Model	Enhancement criteria	parameters	maP Range		Confidence score	
			Min	Max	Min	Max
Faster RCNN	Minmax contrast stretching	IOU=0.75	17.34	55.73	27.56	98.22
YOLO	Minmax contrast stretching	IOU=0.75	19.05	50	35.41	92.55
SSD	Minmax contrast stretching	IOU=0.75	18.23	52.5	32.76	94.4

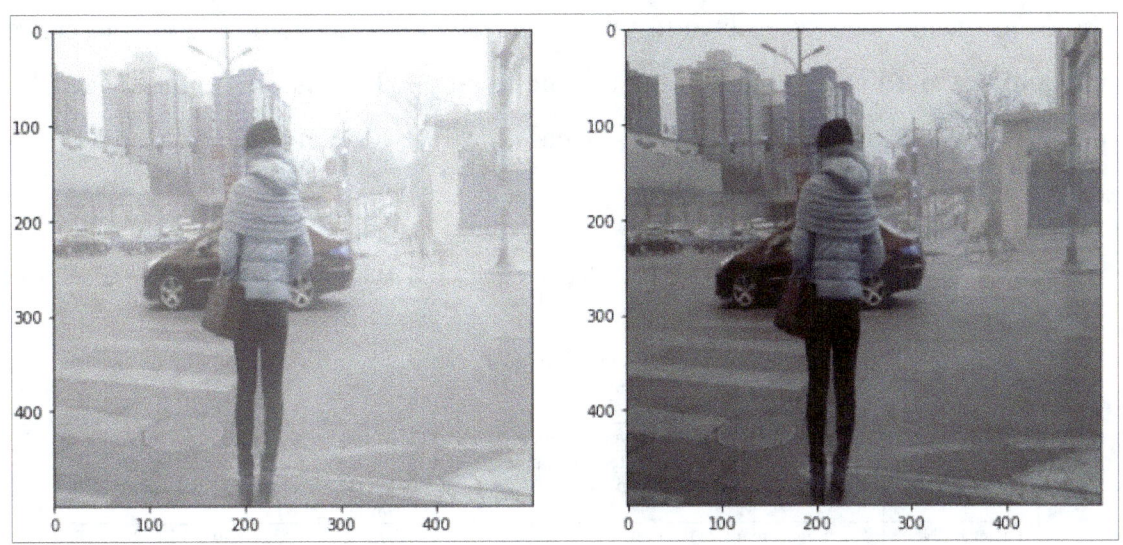

Figure 5.5 Raw image and minmax contrast stretched image

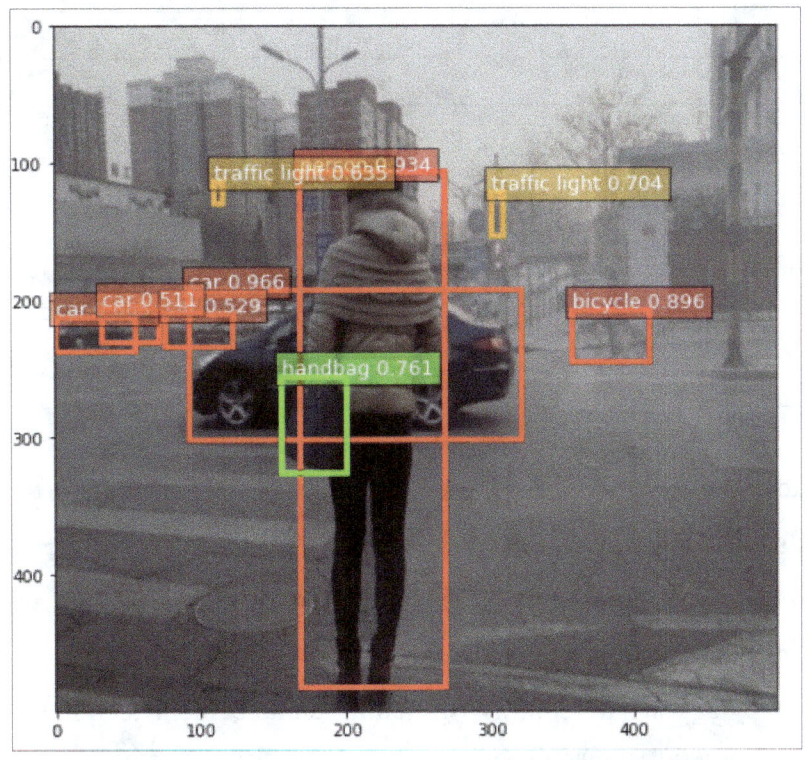

Figure 5.6 Example image with objects detected after Minmax Contrast Stretching

When we performed the experiment for a higher threshold of 0.75. The Faster RCNN models performance improved by 3% and Yolo by 0.5%, and SSD by 0.25%; however, the confidence scores improved by 0.6%, 0.58% and 0.63% for the respective pretrained models.

5.4 Prediction Speed of Models with low light images

The experiments were conducted to understand the speed of prediction of the pretrained model with and without image enhancement techniques applied on the low light images. The detection time without enhancement is used as a baseline reference for comparison with enhancement scenarios.

Table 5.9 Prediction time of models with low light images and enhancement techniques

Model	Enhancement criteria	Prediction time taken per image (for the 125 images of our low light dataset)		
		Average time – when detection is unsuccessful (milliseconds)	Average with successful detection (milliseconds)	Overall time for prediction (milliseconds)
Faster RCNN	No enhancement	30.8	30.1	30.4
YOLO	No enhancement	40.59	40.73	40.6
SSD	No enhancement	25.62	26.31	26.04
Faster RCNN	Gama Correction	29.9	29.03	29.61
YOLO	Gama Correction	39.92	39.85	39.88
SSD	Gama Correction	24.42	24.61	24.54
Faster RCNN	Histogram Equalization	29.33	29.68	29.54
YOLO	Histogram Equalization	39.59	39.05	39.26
SSD	Histogram Equalization	24.77	25.47	25.17
Faster RCNN	Minmax contrast stretching	29.58	28.91	29.18
YOLO	Minmax contrast stretching	40.98	39.94	40.50
SSD	Minmax contrast stretching	24.26	24.99	24.52

The object detection time improved when subjected to enhancement techniques models. When images were subjected to Gamma correction, the prediction speed of Faster RCNN improved by 2.62%, Yolo by 1.73% and SSD by 5.6%. When the images were enhanced with histogram equalization, the low light object detection speed improved by 2.8%. Yolo detected objects in lowlight faster by 3.3%. The contrast stretching enhancement technique improved the detection speed of Faster RCNN by 4%, Yolo by 0.2% and SSD by 5.83%. The pretrained SSD model proved to be the fastest even with low light images among all the three models.

5.5 Summary

The chapter provides a comprehensive overview of the findings and the results of each experiment. We explain the creation of baseline measurement in section 5.2. These initial measurements of pretrained model performance with low light images and without image enhancement techniques are used to compare and identify the improvements of pretrained models with the images subject to enhancement techniques. The results of the enhancement-based experiments are discussed in sections 5.3.1 to 5.3.3 performance with low light. We understood that pretrained models can be used in low light object detection. The findings in multiple experiments also showed that image enhancement techniques improved the model's performance in most of the scenarios. In the final section of the chapter, we discussed the prediction speed of different pretrained models with low light images subject to different enhancement techniques. We observed that enhancing the low light images helps speed up the prediction time of the object detection models. We also identified the fastest model to SSD for low light object detection by comparing the results of our experiments.

Chapter 6   CONCLUSION AND RECOMENDATIONS

6.1   Introduction

In this chapter, we discuss the motivation derived from the literature survey and the conclusions arrived from the implementation of our research work and experiments conducted to understand low light object detection using pretrained models and image enhancement techniques. It outlines the interpretation of the results of our experiments. The chapter also puts some light on the known limitations and improvement areas of our approach. It also explains the key contributions of our research work. The chapter concludes by documenting the future recommendation for our approach. It also provides an overview of the research potential in broader areas of low light computer vision and deep learning.

6.2   Discussion and Conclusion

As we began our study on low light object detection, we found this was an evolving area of research. We also obtained a lot of knowledge from the literature review on low light object detection from the research community. It also provided a motivation to explore low light object detection so that it contributes towards drone-based surveillance, traffic monitoring, human safety, and disaster management scenarios. We understood from several state-of-the-art research that low light object detection had been applied in limited areas such as deepwater exploration, traffic management in tunnels, Traffic monitoring in Rainy and hazy conditions. We also understood that there were opportunities to explore and understand the use and performance of pretrained models in combination with image processing methods like image enhancement techniques has a lot of research potential as it is not totally explored yet. Our work with pretrained models has shown that model's performance and prediction speed has improved in most of the scenarios when image enhancement techniques were applied.

We applied at least three different image enhancement techniques and conducted 24 different experiments with three different pretrained models, namely Faster RCNN, Yolo and SSD with COCO weights. We observed that enhancement techniques applied to low light images improved the performance of the models in scenarios in most of the scenarios. The confidence score of detected objects increased by ~0.5 to 3.5% and mAP by 0.5 to 13%; however, in some scenarios, the percentage of undetected objects increased due to the brute force approach of applying enhancement techniques to all the images. It also shows that with respect to the speed of detection, the SSD model outperformed both Yolo and Faster RCNN under low light object detection conditions. A key finding in the experiments also show that the prediction speed of the model also improved ~0.2 to 5.83%

6.3   Limitations

Some of the key limitations of our approach are, The low light dataset had to be created by manually inspecting images from three different datasets. This is a time-consuming process. Creating annotations and generating ground truth was also a tool based manual approach, which is the second limitation. An automated or mathematical approach of identifying the broader category of low light images is yet to be developed as our current process strongly relies on human judgement and not by data-driven evidence. In our approach, we apply image enhancement in a brute force technique on all the images irrespective of whether the low light images need enhancement. A selective approach intelligent enough to apply the desired enhancement based on the condition of the low light image is not present in our approach. Lastly, the custom dataset created during our study is an imbalanced dataset with a large number of low light images having some common object classes. Though the model is not affected by class imbalance, as we do not use a training-based approach. There may be a slight influence on the interpretation of the model's performance.

6.4   Contribution of Knowledge

The area of our research primarily focuses on object detection in low light conditions. This is one of the rarest attempts to explore the possibility to reuse a pretrained model with low light images without having to train the models with expensive compute. It challenges the computer vision and deep learning community to look at object detection in low light images with a non-conventional approach of training. It also shows opportunities that may open opportunities in the areas of low light computer vision, not limited to object detection where a set of pretrained models (deep learning) in a combination of Image processing or statistical analysis can be applied to other low light computer vision problem domains. Yet another significant contribution of this research work is that the approach promotes the reuse of deep learning knowledge and contributes towards sustainable green or low power machine learning technology initiatives.

6.5 Future Work

Our research has tried to explore the use of pretrained models and use of image processing techniques such as image enhancement to see if it could be used in the context of low light object detection. However, there are few interesting opportunities for further exploration. In our scenario, we have just tried the three models, namely YOLO SSD and Faster RCNN with COCO weights. The research could be further concretized and benchmarked by using trained weights of several other standard datasets and calibrating pretrained model parameters. Another recommendation is to apply a few more image enhancement and image processing techniques to understand the detection performance and pretrained models in the context of low light object detection to understand the minutest details of the detection behaviour. The lakh of good datasets for low light object detection across several domains is still a problem. An interesting initiative is a study to gather datasets and dataset generation techniques for low light object detection. In our experiments, we have studied the model's performance by studying one enhancement technique at a time on low light images to understand the object detection models performance. Alternatively, as an extension of this study, experiments could be conducted to blend multiple image processing techniques based on a low light domain scenario, and the pretrained model performance behaviour can be studied. To conclude, the study should not limit itself to object detection but be generously studied and understood in other computer vision areas such as semantic segmentation and a similar approach be experimented with datasets other than images like videos, lidars and infrared data.

REFERENCES

Arce, G. R. (2005). Nonlinear signal processing: a statistical approach. John Wiley & Sons.

Asyraf, M. S., Isa, I. S., Marzuki, M. I. F., Sulaiman, S. N., & Hung, C. C. (2021). CNN-based YOLOv3 comparison for underwater object detection. Journal of Electrical and Electronic Systems Research (JEESR), 18, 30–37.

Ballard, D. H. (1981). Generalizing the Hough transform to detect arbitrary shapes. Pattern Recognition, 13(2), 111–122.

Buades, A., Coll, B., & Morel, J.-M. (2011). Non-local means denoising. Image Processing On Line, 1, 208–212.

Cai, Z., & Vasconcelos, N. (2018). Cascade r-cnn: Delving into high quality object detection. Proceedings of the IEEE Conference on Computer Vision and Pattern Recognition, 6154–6162.

CALTECH. (n.d.). Caltech Faces 1999. http://www.vision.caltech.edu/html-files/archive.html

Chandler, B., & Mingolla, E. (2016). Mitigation of effects of occlusion on object recognition with deep neural networks through low-level image completion. Computational Intelligence and Neuroscience, 2016.

Chen, X.-Z., Chang, C.-M., Yu, C.-W., & Chen, Y.-L. (2020). A real-time vehicle detection system under various bad weather conditions based on a deep learning model without retraining. Sensors, 20(20), 5731.

cocodataset.org. (n.d.). COCO Annotation format. https://cocodataset.org/#format-data

cvat.org. (2020). Computer Vision Annotation Tool (CVAT). DataPreparation. https://github.com/opencv/cvat

Dongguk university. (n.d.). DNHD-DB1. http://dm.dgu.edu/link.html

Elektra. (n.d.). CVC-14 dataset.

Ethan-Weber. (2020). Incident-Dataset.

https://github.com/ethanweber/IncidentsDataset/tree/master/example_images

Fu, H., Li, Y., Wang, Y., & Li, P. (2018). Maritime ship targets recognition with deep learning. 2018 37th Chinese Control Conference (CCC), 9297–9302.

Girshick, R. (2015). Fast r-cnn. Proceedings of the IEEE International Conference on Computer Vision, 1440–1448.

Graham, D. B., & Allinson, N. M. (n.d.). Characterizing Virtual Eigensignatures for General Purpose Face Recognition. Computer and Systems Sciences, 163, 446–456,.

Han, F., Yao, J., Zhu, H., & Wang, C. (2020). Underwater image processing and object detection based on deep CNN method. Journal of Sensors, 2020.

Harris, C., & Stephens, M. (1988). A combined corner and edge detector. Alvey Vision Conference, 15(50), 10–5244.

Hassaballah, M., Kenk, M. A., Muhammad, K., & Minaee, S. (2020). Vehicle detection and tracking in adverse weather using a deep learning framework. IEEE Transactions on Intelligent Transportation Systems.

He, K., Gkioxari, G., Dollár, P., & Girshick, R. (2017). Mask r-cnn. Proceedings of the IEEE International Conference on Computer Vision, 2961–2969.

He, K., Zhang, X., Ren, S., & Sun, J. (2016). Deep residual learning for image recognition. Proceedings of the IEEE Conference on Computer Vision and Pattern Recognition, 770–778.

Hu, P., & Ramanan, D. (2017). Finding tiny faces. Proceedings of the IEEE Conference on Computer Vision and Pattern Recognition, 951–959.

Hwang, S., Park, J., Kim, N., Choi, Y., & Kweon, I. S. (2015). Multispectral Pedestrian Detection: Benchmark Dataset and Baselines. Proceedings of IEEE Conference on Computer Vision and Pattern Recognition (CVPR).

Jiao, L., Zhang, F., Liu, F., Yang, S., Li, L., Feng, Z., & Qu, R. (2019). A survey of deep learning-based object detection. IEEE Access, 7, 128837–128868.

Lai, K. C., Zhao, J., Liu, D. J., Huang, X. N., & Wang, L. (2021). Research on pedestrian detection using optimized mask R-CNN algorithm in low-light road environment. Journal of

Physics: Conference Series, 1777(1), 12057.

Le, T.-H., Hoang, Q.-V., & Nguyen, M.-Q. (2020). JOINT OPTIMIZATION FOR OBJECT DETECTION IN FOGGY WEATHER CONDITIONS. UTEHY Journal of Science and Technology, 27, 28–33.

Lee, K. B., & Shin, H. S. (2019). An application of a deep learning algorithm for automatic detection of unexpected accidents under bad CCTV monitoring conditions in tunnels. 2019 International Conference on Deep Learning and Machine Learning in Emerging Applications (Deep-ML), 7–11.

Li, B., Ren, W., Fu, D., Tao, D., Feng, D., Zeng, W., & Wang, Z. (2018). Benchmarking single-image dehazing and beyond. IEEE Transactions on Image Processing; IEEE. https://sites.google.com/view/reside-dehaze-datasets/reside-standard

Li, G., Yang, Y., & Qu, X. (2019). Deep learning approaches on pedestrian detection in hazy weather. IEEE Transactions on Industrial Electronics, 67(10), 8889–8899.

Likas, A., Vlassis, N., & Verbeek, J. J. (2003). The global k-means clustering algorithm. Pattern Recognition, 36(2), 451–461.

Liu, L., Ouyang, W., Wang, X., Fieguth, P., Chen, J., Liu, X., & Pietikäinen, M. (2020). Deep learning for generic object detection: A survey. International Journal of Computer Vision, 128(2), 261–318.

Liu, S., & Huang, D. (2018). Receptive field block net for accurate and fast object detection. Proceedings of the European Conference on Computer Vision (ECCV), 385–400.

Liu, W., Anguelov, D., Erhan, D., Szegedy, C., Reed, S., Fu, C.-Y., & Berg, A. C. (2016). Ssd: Single shot multibox detector. European Conference on Computer Vision, 21–37.

Liu, Z., He, Y., Wang, C., & Song, R. (2020). Analysis of the influence of foggy weather environment on the detection effect of machine vision obstacles. Sensors, 20(2), 349.

Loh, Y. P., & Chan, C. S. (2019). Getting to Know Low-light Images with The Exclusively Dark Dataset. Computer Vision and Image Understanding, 178, 30–42. https://doi.org/https://doi.org/10.1016/j.cviu.2018.10.010

Lowe, D. G. (2004). Distinctive image features from scale-invariant keypoints. International Journal of Computer Vision, 60(2), 91–110.

Madhan, E. S., Kannan, K. S., Rani, P. S., Rani, J. V., & Anguraj, D. K. (2021). A distributed submerged object detection and classification enhancement with deep learning. Distributed and Parallel Databases, 1–17.

Michaelis, C., Mitzkus, B., Geirhos, R., Rusak, E., Bringmann, O., Ecker, A. S., Bethge, M., & Brendel, W. (2019). Benchmarking robustness in object detection: Autonomous driving when winter is coming. ArXiv Preprint ArXiv:1907.07484.

Nada, H., Sindagi, V., Zhang, H., & Patel, V. M. (2018). Pushing the Limits of Unconstrained Face Detection: a Challenge Dataset and Baseline Results. ArXiv Preprint ArXiv:1804.10275.

Nath, N. D., & Behzadan, A. H. (2020). Deep convolutional networks for construction object detection under different visual conditions. Frontiers in Built Environment, 6, 97.

Nguyen, H. H. C., Nguyen, D. H., Nguyen, V. L., & Nguyen, T. T. (2020). Smart solution to detect images in limited visibility conditions based convolutional neural networks. International Conference on Computational Collective Intelligence, 641–650.

Nguyen, V. D., Tran, D. D., Tran, M. M., Nguyen, N. M., & Nguyen, V. C. (2020). Robust Vehicle Detection Under Adverse Weather Conditions Using Auto-encoder Feature. International Journal of Machine Learning and Computing, 10(4).

Nie, X., Yang, M., & Liu, R. W. (2019). Deep neural network-based robust ship detection under different weather conditions. 2019 IEEE Intelligent Transportation Systems Conference (ITSC), 47–52.

opencv.org. (n.d.). Open CV Computer Vision library. https://opencv.org/

Pascal-VOC. (2008). Pascal VOC 2008. http://host.robots.ox.ac.uk/pascal/VOC/voc2008/index.html

Radford, A., Metz, L., & Chintala, S. (2015). Unsupervised representation learning with deep convolutional generative adversarial networks. ArXiv Preprint ArXiv:1511.06434.

Redmon, J., Divvala, S., Girshick, R., & Farhadi, A. (2016). You only look once: Unified, real-time object detection. Proceedings of the IEEE Computer Society Conference on Computer Vision and Pattern Recognition, 2016-Decem, 779–788. https://doi.org/10.1109/CVPR.2016.91

Redmon, J., & Farhadi, A. (2018). Yolov3: An incremental improvement. ArXiv Preprint ArXiv:1804.02767.

Ren, S., He, K., Girshick, R., & Sun, J. (2015). Faster r-cnn: Towards real-time object detection with region proposal networks. Advances in Neural Information Processing Systems, 28, 91–99.

Sarin, M., Chandrakar, S., & Patel, R. (2019). Face and human detection in low light for surveillance purposes. 2019 International Conference on Computational Intelligence and Knowledge Economy (ICCIKE), 614–620.

Sasagawa, Y., & Nagahara, H. (2020). Yolo in the dark-domain adaptation method for merging multiple models. European Conference on Computer Vision, 345–359.

Shin, H.-C., Roth, H. R., Gao, M., Lu, L., Xu, Z., Nogues, I., Yao, J., Mollura, D., & Summers, R. M. (2016). Deep convolutional neural networks for computer-aided detection: CNN architectures, dataset characteristics and transfer learning. IEEE Transactions on Medical Imaging, 35(5), 1285–1298.

Simonyan, K., & Zisserman, A. (2015). Very deep convolutional networks for large-scale image recognition The 3rd International Conference on Learning Representations (ICLR2015).

Sindagi, V. A., Oza, P., Yasarla, R., & Patel, V. M. (2020). Prior-based domain adaptive object detection for hazy and rainy conditions. European Conference on Computer Vision, 763–780.

Singh, G., & Singh, A. (2018). Object detection in fog degraded images. International Journal of Computer Science and Information Security (IJCSIS), 16(8).

Solomon, C., & Breckon, T. (2011). Fundamentals of Digital Image Processing: A practical approach with examples in Matlab. John Wiley & Sons.

Uchida, S. (2013). Image processing and recognition for biological images. Development, Growth & Differentiation, 55(4), 523–549.

Volk, G., Müller, S., von Bernuth, A., Hospach, D., & Bringmann, O. (2019). Towards robust CNN-based object detection through augmentation with synthetic rain variations. 2019 IEEE

Intelligent Transportation Systems Conference (ITSC), 285–292.

Wang, J.-G., Chen, S. J., Zhou, L.-B., Wan, K.-W., & Yau, W.-Y. (2018). Vehicle detection and width estimation in rain by fusing radar and vision. 2018 15th International Conference on Control, Automation, Robotics and Vision (ICARCV), 1063–1068.

Wang, Jason, & Perez, L. (2017). The effectiveness of data augmentation in image classification using deep learning. Convolutional Neural Networks Vis. Recognit, 11, 1–8.

Wang, Junhao. (2021). An Improved YOLO Algorithm for Object Detection in All Day Scenarios. International Conference on Knowledge Science, Engineering and Management, 475–486.

Wang, K., & Liu, M. Z. (2020). Object Recognition at Night Scene Based on DCGAN and Faster R-CNN. IEEE Access, 8, 193168–193182.

Wang, X., Shrivastava, A., & Gupta, A. (2017). A-fast-rcnn: Hard positive generation via adversary for object detection. Proceedings of the IEEE Conference on Computer Vision and Pattern Recognition, 2606–2615.

Wu, C.-E., Chan, Y.-M., Chen, C.-H., Chen, W.-C., & Chen, C.-S. (2019). Immvp: An efficient daytime and nighttime on-road object detector. 2019 IEEE 21st International Workshop on Multimedia Signal Processing (MMSP), 1–5.

Wu, Y.-L., Lee, K., & Tang, C.-Y. (2019). Low Visibility Street Scenes Recognition with Augmented Image Sets. 2019 8th International Congress on Advanced Applied Informatics (IIAI-AAI), 438–443.

Wu, Z., Shen, C., & Van Den Hengel, A. (2019). Wider or deeper: Revisiting the resnet model for visual recognition. Pattern Recognition, 90, 119–133.

Xiao, Y., Jiang, A., Ye, J., & Wang, M.-W. (2020). Making of night vision: Object detection under low-illumination. IEEE Access, 8, 123075–123086.

yelon. (2020). Disaster Images Dataset. https://www.kaggle.com/mikolajbabula/disaster-images-dataset-cnn-model

Zhang, S., Zhu, X., Lei, Z., Shi, H., Wang, X., & Li, S. Z. (2017). S3fd: Single shot scale-invariant face detector. Proceedings of the IEEE International Conference on Computer Vision, 192–201.

Zhang, Z., Zhao, L., Liu, Y., Zhang, S., & Yang, J. (2020). Unified Density-Aware Image Dehazing and Object Detection in Real-World Hazy Scenes. Proceedings of the Asian Conference on Computer Vision.

Zheng, H., Liu, J., & Ren, X. (2021). Dim Target Detection Method Based on Deep Learning in Complex Traffic Environment.

Zhiqiang, W., & Jun, L. (2017). A review of object detection based on convolutional neural network. 2017 36th Chinese Control Conference (CCC), 11104–11109.

Zou, Z., Shi, Z., Guo, Y., & Ye, J. (2019). Object Detection in 20 Years: A Survey. ArXiv Preprint ArXiv:1905.05055. http://arxiv.org/abs/1905.05055

APPENDIX A RESEARCH PLAN

The research plan is represented in the form of a Gant chart as shown in figure A.1.1 The plan is represented in terms of weeks and provided for 27 weeks in total. The plan has been changed due the changes brought in the research methodology. As compared to status in the research proposal stage there has been significant progress in area literature survey. The study of image enhancement and denoising techniques have been explored to a great extent.

Post the interim report submission we concretely implemented some image enhancement methods, experimented with pretrained models and found some interesting outcomes. some changes were

made to further refine the research methodology hence some tasks are changed to adapt as per the modified approach. The study has been completed as per the research plan

Figure A.1.0.1 Research Plan

APPENDIX B RESEARCH PROPOSAL

OBJECT DETECTION UNDER POOR LIGHTING CONDITIONS USING DEEP LEARNING

SANATH S SHENOY

Research Proposal

AUGUST 2021

Abstract

In recent years, there is a lot of research being done on object detection using deep learning. As a result, several real-time applications are being developed. These range from pedestrian detection, vehicle detection and counting, visual quality inspection in Industrial production and packaging, damage detection, and face recognition. These are being achieved by using different deep learning architectures such as Convolution Neural Networks and their extensions. Though there has been a lot of progress in these areas, object detection has been challenging in images with low light, poor visibility, or bad weather conditions. The solution to the mentioned scenario is important as it helps in use cases such as drone-based surveillance of important assets and human resources during floods, hurricanes and forest fires, accident avoidance during foggy conditions and improvised detection capabilities in autonomous vehicles during rainy or cloudy conditions. The problem is tried to being solved in both traditional image processing and the use of deep learning. The research using deep learning approaches have been showing promising results. The Proposed study evaluates a set of CNN-based deep learning models like YOLO, Fast RCNN, Faster RCNN, and SSD to choose the suitable deep learning model that can be reused or improvised. Further, this can help detect the objects in low light poor visibility, with improved detection accuracy

Background

Object Detection is the most popular field of computer vision. Some applications of object detection include face detection, pedestrian detection, vehicle detection and tracking on the road. It is also being used extensively in self-driving cars and military drones. Object detection helps identify the type and location of the object in an image or a video. It also provides more information about the object so that the images and videos are understood well semantically (W. Liu et al., 2016). Object detection is also the first step towards advanced computer vision tasks as image or video segmentation, scene understanding, object tracking, image captioning and event detection(L. Liu et al., 2020). The object detection methods can be classified into two types namely traditional and Deep learning-based methods(Zou et al., 2019).

Some of the traditional methods to perform object detection include HOG Transform(Ballard, 1981), Harris Corner detection(Harris & Stephens, 1988) and SIFT(Lowe, 2004). HOG transform works using geometric feature extraction. Harris Corner detection extracts the corner features of two images and uses the correlation between them for detecting the objects. Finally, SIFT uses each feature in the image as an object. It also requires the calculation of key points associated with the location of the features and orientation of features. The algorithm is complex but very robust towards occlusion, rotation, or scaling(Zou et al., 2019). One potential drawback of the traditional methods is their strong dependence on feature engineering.

Currently, deep learning models are used extensively for object detection tasks. This is due to rapid advancement of computational hardware like GPUs and growing interest in the area of computer vision for the use of deep learning methods. The deep learning methods use different variants of Convolution Neural Network for object detection. Depending on the number of stages to accomplish the detection tasks, there are two types of object detection models. They are single-stage and two-stage object detectors. The advantage of single-stage object detectors is that they can infer quickly, and the two-stage object detectors are good at accurate localisation and detection of objects(Jiao et al., 2019). examples of single stage detectors include YOLO (Redmon et al., 2016) and SSD (W. Liu et al., 2016). Similarly, examples of two-stage detectors include Fast RCNN(Girshick, 2015) and Faster RCNN(Ren et al., 2015). This study however only focuses on the use of deep learning-based methods with images that are taken under low light or poor visibility conditions using CNN variants such as YOLO, SSD, Faster-RCNN and Fast-RCNN

Problem Statement

As per (Zhiqiang & Jun, 2017), the object detection mechanism is limited by various factors such as noise, bad resolution, occlusion complex background and other conditions that affect the correctness of detection. Additionally, there has been very limited research on the use of deep learning models to detect objects that are distorted due to rainy, cloudy, foggy or any other low light and unclear environmental conditions that occur due to natural calamities such as hurricanes, forest fires etc. object detection in these scenarios can play a vital role in reducing loss of valuable lives and important assets that affected by the calamity.

Related Work

(Singh & Singh, 2018) explain the main factors contributing to poor object detection performance with videos and images. These mainly include poor visibility, Hazy or fogginess in the image or the video. They suggest preprocessing the image using a guided filter and integrating Discrete Wavelet Transformation methods with the deep learning CNN architecture(Shin et al., 2016). The approach improves the detection performance by reducing the mean squared errors and improving the PSNR, Image information entropy significantly.

(Nie et al., 2019) use YoloV3(Redmon & Farhadi, 2018) deep learning architecture to detect ships in bad weather. They try to understand whether Image enhancement techniques or a training technique with both good and bad whether images improve the detection performance. The findings help conclude that by combining degraded images and good images in the training phase, the model can improve the ship detection performance under bad weather significantly when compared to applying certain image enhancement techniques as a preprocessing step.

(G. Li et al., 2019) try to detect pedestrians in a hazy, low light image by modifying yolo deep learning architecture. It uses depth-wise convolution instead of the standard convolution technique. This helps to increase the speed of computation. It also uses a linear activation function instead of relu to minimize information loss. Additionally, a concept of priory boxes is introduced, which uses different sized boxes. The sizes are determined using K-Means(Likas et al., 2003) so that the network needs to learn to mark pedestrians or objects from the scratch. The modified architecture improved the detection performance by 4% from 79% to 83% and processing speed from 22 frames per second to 159 frames per second.

(Chen et al., 2020) uses a deep learning model for image correction contrast adjustments and noise removal known as visibility complementation module. The processed output is passed to the Yolo network for vehicle detection. The combined architecture is trained for a combination of different types of videos containing glare, hazy and rainy environments. The performance of detection is verified to be improved by 5% and the performance of detection in a rainy condition by 50%. The research further emphasizes the need for improvements and techniques to deal with more hazy and complex conditions.

(Z. Liu et al., 2020) use Faster RCNN to detect vehicles under different lighting conditions such as sunny, light, medium and heavy fog conditions. The model's recall is 91.55% for sunny weather and ranges from 72.54 to 57.75% for light, heavy fog conditions. The paper tries to support the use of deep learning models such as Faster RCNN to sufficient evidence so that it could be used in real-time for vehicle detection in foggy conditions and extend the use to pedestrian detection.

(Asyraf et al., 2021) experiment with different YOLOv3 architecture variants to detect animals deep under the sea. They also highlight the main challenge that can affect the performance of detection is degraded visibility in the image. As a result, the experiments are conducted by subjecting the images to preprocessing and augmentation. Different YOLO variants are trained and compared against each other to understand the detection capability of each model.

(Lai et al., 2021) tries to improve pedestrian detection in low light conditions by modifying the Mask R-CNN(He et al., 2017) network. It introduces a fusion layer to enhance the region sensitivity and instance segmentation capability. As a result, the network's detection accuracy improves by 4.66%. The network is trained with varied image sizes and tested in a real environment as part of the electric vehicle to validate the finding.

Research Question

The research questions for the study are to understand the following

- How do standard deep learning object detection models perform the detection task in low light conditions?
- Can standard deep learning object detection models be improvised, modified or combined for better object detection accuracy and speed under low light conditions?
- What are the factors that contribute to the detection accuracy and speed of the deep learning models in low light conditions?

Aim and Objectives

The aim of this research is to propose the use of deep learning models to detect objects in poor light or bad weather conditions. The research will be of great help to identify critical assets that need quick response, save lives, and manage disasters. These include poor visibility conditions that occur as a natural phenomenon like rainy, cloudy, or foggy conditions during a hurricane, poor lighting conditions arising due to forest fire or earthquakes.

The research objectives on the aim of this study are as follows:
- Preprocess the images so that they are suitable for training with the deep learning model.
- Identify the objects within an image using pre-trained deep learning models
- Train the deep learning model from the scratch using different images and identify objects.
- Systematically understand the performance of detection of both pre-trained models and models trained from scratch.
- Modify the model or its parameters to improve the detection accuracy and speed.
- Compare the performance with at least three models to validate the detection performance

Significance of the Study

The research tries to leverage the capability of computer vision and deep learning to identify objects of interest in images taken at low light bad weather or poor visibility condition. It can be in various real-life scenarios. For example, in times of calamities and Natural disasters, the research can help identify, track and analyse critical assets or human resources. It can also help in achieving this without having to manually visit these areas which can cause potential threat to the life of rescue personal. It can be used for remotely monitoring, tracking and decision making. This can help save time and resources. As the approach uses simple RGB images, it provides a potential low-cost alternative as compared to sensor-based approaches. The research can also be deployed in unmanned drones for surveillance where lighting conditions are bad. It can also be used with self-driving vehicles to detect different objects of interest such as obstacles, signals humans and signs in low light conditions. These are some examples that clearly quantify the significance and benefits of the study, which in turn contribute to advancement in technology, save human life and time.

Scope of the Study

The scope of the research is to use deep learning-based models for object detection of images in poor lighting and bad weather conditions. The study is limited to images that are taken in rainy, foggy, cloudy, bad weather conditions. It also includes detection in hazy and bad visibility conditions taken from outdoors during hurricanes, earthquakes, forest fires and floods. It does not focus on object detection in dark spaces like deep ocean underwater lighting conditions, bad lighting conditions inside the natural caves or manmade buildings. It also does not focus on extremely dark and no light conditions or the lighting environments at a night setting. Additionally, the focus of the study is limited to the use of CNN based deep learning models such YOLO, Faster RCNN, Fast RCNN(Girshick, 2015) and SSD, improvising and tuning the parameter or the network architecture that is best suited for object detection in the context of the low light and bad weather conditions.

Research Methodology

- Overview of the methodology

The research will be conducted to detect objects in low light or bad weather conditions. The research methodology will be followed as per the steps depicted in figure 8.1. This includes loading and understanding the Image dataset, annotating the objects of interest, preprocessing the images, splitting the dataset into two parts namely training and validation sets. The research is further conducted to understand the object detection performance with pretrained CNN models using the validation set. The study is also

Figure B.1.0.1 Flow chart of the Proposed Research Methodology

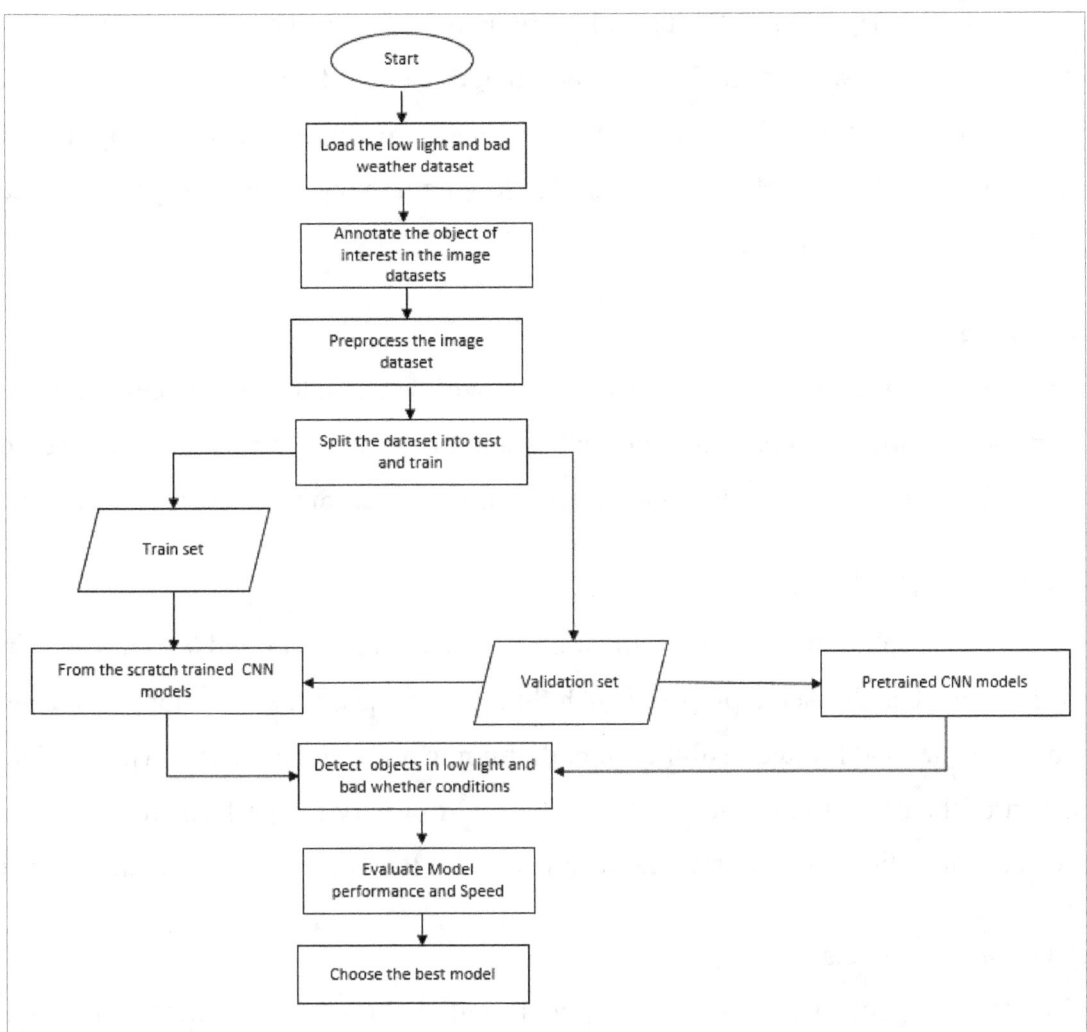

performed by training a set of CNN models from the scratch and modifying their architecture and parameters. Finally, the model performance and speed are compared using the validation set of images to choose the best model. The findings such as benefit gains or drawbacks are summarized to conclude the research study.

- Dataset Description

The low light bad weather datasets are not available as standard datasets, so we collect these from various online image sources. These include the Kaggle disaster image dataset(yelon, 2020), low-light images from GitHub(Ethan-Weber, 2020), The Pascal VOC 2008 dataset((Pascal-VOC, 2008) low-light images and the Reside dataset(B. Li et al., 2018). The disaster image dataset consists of 4500 images of 4 categories. These include hurricanes, earthquake floods and Forest-fire. These are RGB images with 96 dpi with various resolutions. The GitHub low light image repository consists of 4 low light and bad weather images captured during natural calamities. The Pascal VOC 2008 has around 70 low light images which are helpful for our study. Finally, the Reside dataset is an extensive collection containing low light, hazy images of types synthetic and real for both indoor and outdoor scenarios.

- Pre-processing

The low light bad weather dataset used for the study will be subject to preprocessing steps such as converting to uniform size denoising, normalisation and adjusting the brightness and contrast of the images are made suitable for use with deep learning for learning or detection purposes.

- Splitting Data into Train and Validation Sets

The image dataset is split into train and validation sets. The ratio is around 75% for training and 25% for validation. The dataset is prepared such that it contains all the variations of images with low light bad weather and limited visibility in both training and validation sets. The validation set is a small part of the dataset unlabeled under study used to verify the performance of the models with unseen data and choose the best model with respect to the detection performance and speed.

- Use of Pretrained Models

A set of pretrained general-purpose CNN models will be used to understand the detection performance and speed in the context of the low light and bad weather datasets used in this research. This is also used as a reference to understand the detection behavior

- Choice of Models for the study
    - Yolo variants use Regression as their core idea to solve the object detection problem. They use a Single CNN to predict the bounding boxes and probabilities of the object classes associated with the box at the same time. It does not process the image in parts instead uses the whole image during its training and testing phase. The model is of particular interest for the study due to its simplicity in the architecture and speed of detection .it also understands the features in a generic way and does not have problems with background scenes.

- SSD uses small convolution filters and a small set of default boxes .it also uses feature maps of different scales to detect objects for different aspect ratios. Additionally, the model uses a novel loss function. The loss function is the weighted sum of localisation and confidence loss. The model is important for our study as it can detect objects in images of very low resolution. It also provides a good balance between accuracy and speed of detection.

- The Fast RCNN uses an image and a set of region proposals as input. It uses convolution and pooling to generate the feature map. It also uses a technique called ROI pooling for extracting the features from the feature map. The ROI pooling layer is used to extract small feature maps of fixed spatial dimensions from the areas of the valid region of interest. These features are then processed by a set of fully connected layers to two provide two outputs. The first output provides the probability of each class of the object being identified. The second output contains four values corresponding to the position of the bounding box for each object class identified. The network also uses softmax instead of SVM for classification. The network is of significance in the study as it uses the image directly as input and Idea of Convolution to restrict the number of selective searches to one per image .it has better quality object detection capabilities and use less disk space when compared to RCNN.

- The Faster RCNN contains two parts. The first one is Convolution Neural Network that creates Region Proposal also known as the RPN Region Proposal Network. The RPN takes images of varied sizes and outputs region proposals and a confidence score. The Second part is Fast RCNN which uses the region proposal to predict objects. The model uses translation-invariant anchors and pyramid of filters. The computations are also shared between the network, making it faster than the Fast R-CNN. This model is important for our study as it helps detect objects in different orientations or translation conditions with good accuracy.

- Training Evaluation and optimisation of models and their parameters

The CNN-based deep learning models such as YOLO, SSD, Faster RCNN and Fast RCNN are trained with the dataset chosen in the context of our research using the training set. Then, they are iteratively tested with the validation set to understand the detection performance. Finally, the best performing network with respect to the validation set is chosen for further modification of layers and tuning of parameters. As part of our research, we would use recall, precision, average precision and mean absolute precision for measuring the performance of object detection as this is a standard practice. For detection speed, we would use time in seconds for every image processed.

Requirements Resources

As part of the study, we plan the use of both software and hardware components. The software components include python 3.8, TensorFlow GPU version ranging 2.0 <= 2.2, MXNET, GluonCV, Cudnn, OpenCV, Sklearn and skimage, pillow, Jupyter notebook, Anaconda environment and optionally Tensorboard. The operating system used for this study can be Ubuntu Linux 18.04 LTS and above. The hardware components include using a fairly good cloud Virtual Machine (VM) with Intel CPU with 64bit architecture. The machine should also have a Nvidia GPU that can be used to train the deep learning model. The VM setup needs to have a minimum of 16GB of RAM and Solid-State Drive storage. The virtual machine instance should be accessible remotely via SSH protocol, Remote Desktop and VNC Connectivity.

Research Plan

The research plan is represented in the form of a Gant chart as shown in figure 9.1. The plan is represented in terms of weeks and provided for 27 weeks in total.

Figure B.1.0.2 Initial Research Plan

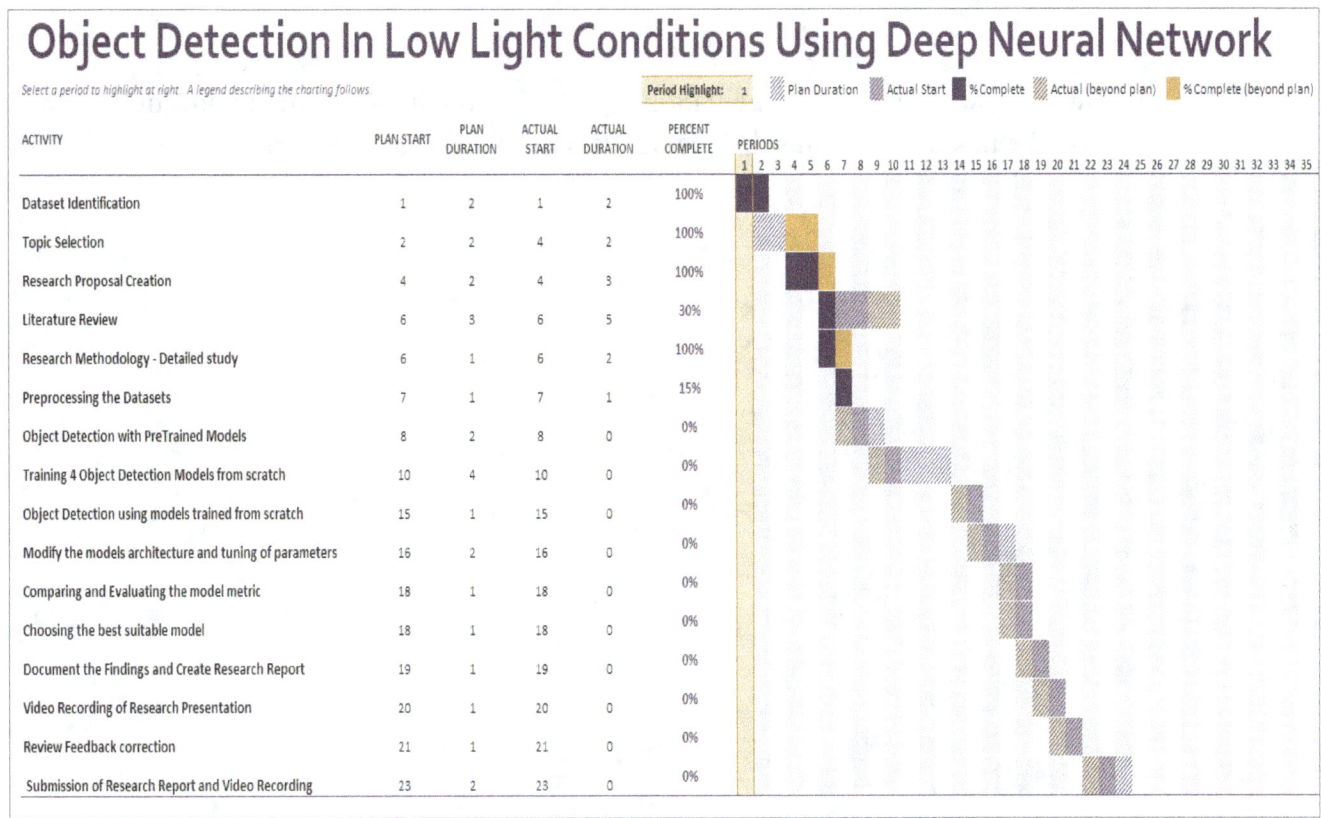

APPENDIX C CODE ON LOW-LIGHT OBJECT DETECTION

The source code of our implementation can be found in the GitHub location as a [Jupyter Notebook](). the link also contains the custom dataset which we have created.

APPENDIX D ETHICS FORMS